CityPack
Singapore

VIVIEN LYTTON

Vivien Lytton lived in Singapore in the mid-1990s, working in publishing, project managing illustrated books on Southeast Asia. She maintains a close interest in the region, and in Singapore – one of the world's great crossroads – in particular.

City-centre
map on inside
back cover

AA Publishing

Contents

About this book

KEY TO SYMBOLS

- map reference on the fold-out map accompanying this book (see below)
- address
- telephone number
- opening times
- restaurant or café on premises or near by
- nearest Metro (underground) train station
- nearest overground train station
- nearest bus route
- nearest riverboat or ferry stop
- facilities for visitors with disabilities
- admission charge
- other nearby places of interest
- tours, lectures, or special events
- ➤ cross-reference (see below)
- tourist information

ORGANISATION

CityPack Singapore's six sections cover the six most important aspects of your visit to Singapore:

- Singapore – the city and its people
- Itineraries, walks and excursions – how to organise your time
- The top 25 sights to visit, arranged from west to east across the city
- Features about different aspects of the city that make it special
- Detailed listings of restaurants, hotels, shops and nightlife
- Practical information

In addition, text boxes provide fascinating extra facts and snippets, highlights of places to visit and invaluable practical advice.

CROSS-REFERENCES

To help you make the most of your visit, cross-references, indicated by ➤ , show you where to find additional information about a place or subject.

MAPS

- **The fold-out map** in the wallet at the back of the book is a comprehensive street plan of Singapore. All the map references given in the book refer to this map. For example, the Sri Mariamman Temple on South Bridge Road has the following information: bII/E8 – indicating the grid square of the enlarged inset map (bII) and that of the main map (E8) in which the Temple will be found.
- **The Singapore Island and city-centre maps** found on the inside front and back covers of the book itself are for quick reference. They show the Top 25 Sights, described on pages 24–48, which are clearly plotted by number (1 – 25, not page number) from west to east.

PRICES

Where appropriate, an indication of the cost of an establishment is given by **£** signs: **£££** denotes higher prices, **££** denotes average prices, while **£** denotes lower charges.

SINGAPORE
life

INTRODUCING SINGAPORE

Singapore River comes to life

In recent years, ambitious projects to develop the banks of the Singapore River as eating and entertainment areas have been completed. As a result, after decades of being a backwater following the development of the modern port areas, the river bank is once more bustling. The carefully restored and re-created shop houses and warehouses along Boat Quay, Clarke Quay and the upper river now offer a wide selection of theme restaurants and shops, tempting tourists and office workers alike.

In many senses Singapore is a model city. It is relatively small, as world capitals go, overwhelmingly modern, faultlessly clean and with few shortcomings when it comes to the fabric of the city. Its many hotels, its transport and communications systems, its myriad restaurants and shops and its economic activities are diverse and impressive and seemingly Western. But if you scratch below the surface you find a very Asian city. It is a mosaic of Asian peoples and influences. In spite of the island's rapid development in the last 40 years and the cityscape of tower blocks, highways and glitzy shopping centres, pockets of old Singapore can be found, relieving the modern monotony. The core of old Chinatown still hums with small-time traders, occasional backstreet Chinese opera performances can be happened upon, Indian fortune-tellers give pavement consultations, Malay foodstalls appear at dusk near mosques in the month of Ramadan, gin and tonic is still taken on the veranda of the Cricket Club, and small oases of undeveloped tropical forest and mangrove provide some respite from the concrete jungle.

This small island, located just over 100km north of the Equator, is tropical – very tropical – with average humidity always well above 90 per cent and the temperature range rarely wavering from a noon-time high of 31°C and a night-time low of 24°C. Despite the surge in construction in recent decades, urban areas are strikingly green, with both tree-lined avenues and small parks commonplace. Apart from some of Southeast

Singapore port handles more tonnage than any other port in the world

Asia's tallest buildings and the occasional hill, Singapore is very flat, with little of the island above 15m. The Singapore River still bisects the centre of the city, with the core of the original colonial government buildings and the Padang – the colonial 'village green' – on the north bank and remnants of the old areas originally settled by Indians, Arab and Malay inhabitants beyond. To the south the main business district is found, with Chinatown hard on its heels to the west. Today the mouth of the river is dwarfed by the skyscrapers of Raffles Place and confined by huge land reclamations to the north, east and south. Another distinctive area is Orchard Road, the city's premier shopping street. Here, in the glamour of shopping centre after shopping centre, the world's goods can be bought.

Beyond this central city core are the extensive residential and industrial areas, in particular a number of huge 'new town' estates – block upon block of medium- and high-rise apartments. All these towns are self-sufficient, offering good shopping, recreational and educational amenities, and most are linked to the centre by a modern underground railway known as the Mass Rapid Transit (MRT). Originally developed as public housing, the majority of homes are now privately owned and although the tower blocks may make a stiflingly dull, 'toy town' environment, it is one largely devoid of crime and vandalism.

The population of Singapore is predominantly Chinese, who comprise three-quarters of the city's inhabitants. Many only arrived three or four generations ago from provinces in southern China and from Malacca. Malays make up the next largest sector of the population and Indians less than a tenth. As a result of Singapore's colonial and trading history and importance today as a regional capital, there are also numerous Eurasians and expatriate workers from all over the world. This diversity of races, religions and creeds is best exemplified by Singapore's many festivals and traditions (▶ 22, 80–1).

Lion dance at Haw Par Villa (Tiger Balm Gardens)

Gone shopping

Shopping, along with eating, is a national obsession, and designer labels are highly prized in Singapore s largely af uent and materialistic society. Although the early 1998 economic downturn cast a damper on consumer spending in many of the city s gleaming shopping centres, retailers of exclusive clothing, jewellery and accessories still abound. On weekend afternoons Orchard Road, nicknamed the catwalk , becomes the place to be seen dressed up in the latest fashion. But be warned, Singapore is no longer a bargain basement: prices for many goods, in many outlets, are comparable with those in London, New York and Sydney.

SINGAPORE IN FIGURES

GEOGRAPHY	• Singapore is a small island 137km north of the Equator – only 650sq km. It measures 42km east–west and 23km north–south • It has a tropical climate with virtually no seasonal differences. The maximum daily temperature is 35°C and the minimum 24°C. Humidity is usually over 90 per cent and the annual rainfall is around 2,400mm • Singapore's highest peak is Bukit Timah (163m), located in the middle of the island
POPULATION	• Population growth: 1819 500 1901 230,000 1820 5,000 1911 312,000 1824 10,000 1957 1,470,000 1860 80,000 1996 3,045,000 • Population composition: Chinese 77%; Malay 14%; Indian 7%; others 2% • Religious make-up of the population: Taoist 29%; Buddhist 27%; Muslim 15%; Christian 11%; Hindu 4%; other/none 14% • Today's population density: 4,200 per sq km – one of the highest in the world
LANGUAGES	• There are four official languages: English, Malay, Mandarin and Tamil
ECONOMY	• Some 87% of the population lives in Housing Development Board apartment blocks – built within the last 30 years • Per capita income has grown from US$300 in 1965 to US$27,000 in 1997 • In 1996, 7,290,000 visitors came to Singapore and 24,500,000 passengers used the airport • It has the busiest port in terms of shipping tonnage, used by nearly 400 shipping lines and with links to over 600 ports worldwide • In 1998 Singapore spent almost as much on defence and security as it did on education
DISTANCES	• London 10,850km Paris 10,730km Frankfurt 10,270km New York 15,320km Sydney 6,290km Hong Kong 2,756km

SINGAPORE PEOPLE

LEE KUAN YEW

Today, Senior Minister Lee Kuan Yew is Singapore's most famous citizen. A lawyer by training, he is credited with transforming Singapore, almost single-handedly, from Third World trading port to highly developed nation – all within 35 years. He helped form the People's Action Party in 1954 and was elected Prime Minister at the age of 36 in 1959. Renowned for his discipline, hard work and intolerance, he encouraged education, housing, infrastructure and manufacturing (though not criticism and dissension), with amazing results. During his premiership the economic growth rate averaged 9 per cent per year, literacy rates rose to more than 90 per cent, and today there is full employment. Despite stepping aside as Prime Minister in 1990, Lee Kuan Yew remains active and vocal as Senior Minister. He is very much sought after by governments and organisations abroad for advice and comment.

Lee Kuan Yew

PHILIP JEYARETNAM

Cambridge-trained lawyer Philip Jeyaretnam is also one of Singapore's most promising young writers. He first started writing while doing his compulsory two-year national service stint, after discovering that one way of beating the tedium was to describe his experiences in the minutest detail. His writing, not surprisingly, focuses on Singapore. *First Loves*, his first work and some say his best, is a collection of short stories describing the adventures of a young dreamer growing up in practical Singapore.

CLAIRE CHIANG

Claire Chiang is a woman very much in the public eye. A sociologist and noted champion of women's issues, she is currently juggling her work as manager of the family-owned Banyan Tree Gallery with her roles as President of the Society Against Family Violence and as a nominated member of parliament. She has researched extensively into Singapore's migrant history and has written a book documenting the stories of little-known migrants from China.

Singapore girl

Singapore Airlines is consistently voted one of the world's best airlines. The airline's stewardesses play no small part in this achievement. Undeniably attractive, well trained and attentive, they are distinctively attired in batik and have become such a strong symbol of the airline, and of Singapore itself, that at one time there was even a representative waxwork figure in Madam Tussaud's, London.

A CHRONOLOGY

3rd century AD	Singapore first mentioned as Pu luo chung – 'the island at the end of the peninsula' – in Chinese seafaring records
Late 13th century	Marco Polo notes a thriving city, possibly a satellite town of the Sumatran Srivijayan empire which flourished between the 7th and 14th centuries. This city could have been Singapore, or Temasek as it was then known. The Malay Annals of the 16th century – Sejara Melayu – document a 13th-century Singapura, meaning 'Lion City'
Late 14th century	At this time the island's ruler, Parameswara, is forced to flee to Malacca. For the next 400 years Singapore is all but abandoned except for pirates and fishermen
1819	Stamford Raffles founds Singapore as a trading post midway between India and China and close to the newly acquired British colonies of the Dutch East Indies
1826	Together with Penang and Malacca, Singapore becomes part of the Straits Settlements
1867	Designated a Crown Colony under direct British rule. With growing trade in tin and plantation crops, the introduction of steamships and its strategic location, Singapore becomes a hub of international trade
1870s	Tens of thousands of immigrants from South China begin arriving in Singapore. They work in the shipyards and rubber plantations and as small traders
1874	Botanic Gardens officially open on a new site at the end of Holland Road
1887	Propagation of the first rubber trees in Asia by Henry Ridley, Director of the Botanic Gardens. Raffles Hotel is established
1921	The threat of Japan's increasing military might initiates the construction of coastal defences

1942	Singapore falls to the Japanese on 15 February. It is renamed Syonan-to, 'Light of the South'
1945	Lord Louis Mountbatten receives the Japanese surrender on 12 September
1954	Singapore's first elections – a Legislative Council is elected to advise the Governor
1955	Lee Kuan Yew founds the People's Action Party (PAP). Legislative Assembly set up. David Marshall becomes Singapore's first Chief Minister
1957	Malaya becomes independent on 31 August
1959	The PAP forms the first government. Lee Kuan Yew is appointed Prime Minister
1963	Singapore forms the Federation of Malaysia with Malaya, Sarawak and North Borneo
1965	Leaves the Federation on 9 August and becomes an independent sovereign nation
1966	Singapore dollar becomes the official currency
1967	Founder member of the Association of South-East Asian Nations (ASEAN)
1968	British military withdrawal announced and Singapore sets up its own air force and navy
1977	1,165ha of land is reclaimed from the sea for businesss and residential use
1981	Changi Airport opens
1988	Singapore's Mass Rapid Transit (MRT) system is inaugurated
1990	Lee Kuan Yew steps aside and Goh Chok Tong becomes Prime Minister
1993	Singapore's first presidential election. Former cabinet minister Ong Teng Cheong is elected

PEOPLE & EVENTS FROM HISTORY

Fast work

It took Raffles just one week to conclude a deal with the local sultans to lease the island and appoint William Farquhar as Governor. Within four months more than 4,000 people had been attracted to settle. By the time Raffles returned in 1822, more than 3,000 vessels had registered at the port and the population had expanded to 10,000.

Japanese occupation

In 1942 the Japanese launched their attack on Singapore from Johor Bahru, at the southern tip of the Malay Peninsula, having already overrun Malaya within six weeks. Despite being outnumbered by three to one, it took the Japanese army just a few days to gain control in Singapore, during which time tens of thousands of British, Indian and Australian troops were killed or wounded. During the Occupation up to 50,000 Chinese men were executed and the Allied troops were interned or dispatched to work on the infamous Burma Railway.

RAFFLES – FOUNDER OF SINGAPORE

Thomas Stamford Raffles was born in 1781, the son of a sea captain. He started work at the age of 14 as a clerk in the East India Company in London. In 1805 he was appointed Assistant Secretary for Penang, then in 1811 Lieutenant-Governor of Java and in 1818 Lieutenant-Governor of Bencoolen (now Bengkulu), a port in south-west Sumatra. He soon realised that a port more advantageously located than either Penang or Bencoolen would be a great benefit to trading interests in the region, and in 1819 he landed in Singapore and secured the island as a free trade port for the British.

In 1822, plagued by ill health, Raffles resigned and set sail for Singapore. 'It would be difficult to name a place on the face of the globe with brighter prospects or more pleasant satisfaction', he wrote. In the nine months he spent in Singapore he drafted a constitution, set up a land registry and drew up a town plan giving each race an area in which to settle. But his life was dogged with misfortune. His first wife and four of his children died in Java and Sumatra, he received limited recognition from the East India Company, and on his final return to England his scientific collection was lost in a ship's fire. In England, still suffering bad health, he was active in the Royal Society and helped found the London Zoological Gardens. Then, with so much achieved but many more aspirations, he died, just one day before his 46th birthday.

GOING REGIONAL

Singapore's aim to expand its economy, by increasing business activity with neighbouring economies, is already being realised. In 1994 it signed an agreement to develop a 70sq km industrial township near Shanghai, China. Much of the infrastructure is being supplied and built by Singapore companies. In the same year a Singapore consortium started building a S$250 million technology park in Bangalore, India. Singapore is involved in similar developments in Vietnam, Thailand and Indonesia.

SINGAPORE
how to organise your time

ITINERARIES

Many central sights are within walking distance of each other, but the heat
and humidity make even the shortest of walks sticky and tiring. Try to do
most of your outdoor sightseeing before 11AM and after 4PM. And don't do
too much without stopping for a drink or a blast of air-conditioned comfort
– neither is hard to find.

ITINERARY ONE	**SINGAPORE'S COLONIAL HEART**
	Many of Singapore's grand colonial institutions are to be found around the Padang – the colonial city equivalent of the village green
Morning	Singapore History Museum (► 39)
	Coffee at the Substation café, Armenian Street or MPH bookshop opposite
	Walk down North Bridge Road passing St Andrew's Cathedral
	Head down High Street to see Parliament House and Victoria Concert Hall and Theatre, and the Singapore Cricket Club
	Turn left down St Andrew's Road past the Supreme Court, City Hall and Padang (► 43)
Lunch	Raffles Hotel, Beach Road (► 44)
Afternoon	Raffles Museum
	Raffles City Shopping Centre
ITINERARY TWO	**CHINATOWN & THE SINGAPORE RIVER**
	The overflowing shops and stalls and the old-fashioned commerce of Chinatown is a great contrast to the pristine regeneration developments of the Singapore River
Morning	People's Park Complex, Eu Tong Sen Street
	Coffee at a Chinese coffee-shop in People's Park hawker centre or Trengganu Street (► 34)
	Sri Mariamman Temple (► 36)
	Turn down Boon Tat Street to Robinson Road
Lunch	Lau Pa Sat (Telok Ayer Market)
Afternoon	Head down Robinson Road, across Raffles Place and down Bonham Street to reach Boat Quay (► 41). Take in the views to Raffles' landing place and Empress Place

ITINERARY THREE	**LITTLE INDIA & ARAB STREET** *Singapore's multiculturalism has been a feature of its population from earliest times*
Morning	Serangoon Road (Little India) (➤ 40) Coffee at one of the stalls in the colourful Zhujiao Centre Market (K K Market) Walk down Serangoon Road passing Sri Veeramakaliamman Temple and Sri Srinivasa Perumal Temple Retrace your steps on the other side of Serangoon Road, exploring side streets
Lunch	Vegetarians can try Madras New Woodlands Restaurant, 14 Upper Dickson Road, or non-vegetarians Maharaja's Kitchen, 42 Veerasamy Road
Afternoon	Walk from Sungei Road to Arab Street Down Arab Street, turn left at Baghdad Street Bussorah Street and Sultan Mosque (➤ 46) Retrace your steps. Take Beach Road up to Raffles Hotel and relax with a drink
ITINERARY FOUR	**THE BOTANIC GARDENS & ORCHARD ROAD** *An hour's stroll in the beautiful, quiet gardens is a gentle way to start the day and good preparation for the rigours of shopping on Orchard Road*
Morning	Botanic Gardens – the main entrance is at the bottom of Cluny Road (➤ 30) Coffee at the Taman Serasi hawker centre outside the main gates Walk down Napier Road and turn left into Tanglin Road Continue down Tanglin Road to Tanglin Shopping Centre
Lunch	Head down Orchard Road and left up Scotts Road (via footbridge) to the Goodwood Park hotel (➤ 82), an excellent lunch stop
Afternoon	Return to Orchard Road and turn left into the shopping bustle, keeping a lookout for Tangs, Ngee Ann City (➤ 32) and Centrepoint

15

WALKS

A WALK ROUND SINGAPORE'S HISTORIC CORE

Allow a full day for this walk, with breaks for meals, or choose part of it for a shorter walk.

Morning For an all-day walk, start as early as possible with coffee at the Maxwell Road Hawker Centre. Walk down South Bridge Road to Smith Street on your left; take this street and return to South Bridge Road via Pagoda Street (➤ 34). Notice the renovated Chinese shop houses (ground-floor shops with dwellings above). Visit the Sri Mariamman Temple – Singapore's oldest Hindu temple. Cross over and take Ann Siang Hill, then turn left down Club Street. Turn right at Cross Street and left into Telok Ayer Street. Fuk Tak Ch'i Temple now houses a museum, while Far East Square and China Square present numerous eating and shopping opportunities. Turn right down Cheang Hong Lim Street and then left at the end. Follow Cecil Street and D'Almeida Street into Raffles Place. Continue straight into Bonham Street and left into Boat Quay. Have lunch at one of the many restaurants.

Cavenagh Bridge

Afternoon Follow the riverbank down to the Cavenagh Bridge. Cross over and pass Empress Place and the Victoria Concert Hall and Theatre. On your right is the Singapore Cricket Club (note that non-members are not admitted and to this day one bar even remains off-limits to female members!).

Cross over High Street and take St Andrew's Road, passing the Supreme Court, City Hall and St Andrew's Cathedral on your left. The Padang is on your right. After Raffles City you come next to Raffles Hotel – an ideal place for afternoon tea. Alternatively, try Ah Teng's Bakery or the Seah Street Deli (you will need to walk

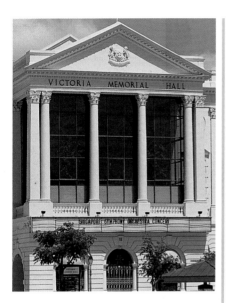

Victoria Concert Hall and Theatre

INFORMATION

Morning
Distance 5km
Time 3 hours
Start point Maxwell Road Hawker Centre
🚇 bIII/E8
Ⓜ Tanjong Pagar MRT
End point Boat Quay
🚇 dl/E7
Ⓜ Raffles Place MRT

Afternoon
Distance 5km
Time 3 hours
Start point Boat Quay
🚇 dl/E7
Ⓜ Raffles Place MRT
End point Victoria Street
🚇 F6
Ⓜ Bugis MRT

Evening
Distance 3km
Time 1 hour
Start and end point Serangoon Road
🚇 E5
Ⓜ Bugis MRT

through the hotel and its shopping arcade to reach these cafés). Continue along Beach Road. Turn left into Arab Street, right into Baghdad Street and left into Bussorah Street. Sultan Mosque, at the end of this street, is a magnificent sight. Facing the mosque, take the side street to your left and then head right up Arab Street to the crossroads with Victoria Street. Here you can wander around a number of streets lined with old shops selling cloth and handicrafts. At this point you'll need a break and probably a shower back at your hotel.

Evening Take in Little India, starting at the beginning of Serangoon Road with the market on your left and the Little India Arcade on the right. Taking side-street detours (including a left up Buffalo Road and then a right into Race Course Road to find the banana-leaf restaurants ➤ 63), walk up as far as Serangoon Plaza. Walk back down, enjoying the bustling side streets. You'll be tempted for dinner long before you reach the beginning of Serangoon Road – guaranteed!

17

EVENING STROLLS

Night-time splendour of Raffles Hotel

Singapore is one of the world's safest cities. There is no need to worry, beyond taking normal precautions, wherever you find yourself wandering, day or night. Taking advantage of the slightly cooler conditions in the evenings is also a good reason to do more than just sit in an air-conditioned restaurant.

COLONIAL SINGAPORE: RAFFLES HOTEL TO THE SINGAPORE RIVER

From the main entrance of Raffles Hotel (► 44) turn right and walk towards the Padang (► 43). On your left is the war memorial. Continue down St Andrew's Road. The newly rebuilt Recreation Club on your left was originally established for Eurasians, who were not allowed into the Cricket Club at the opposite end of the Padang. Passing St Andrew's Cathedral, City Hall and the Supreme Court on your right, you come to the Cricket Club. Cross over here and go down Parliament Lane, with Parliament House on your right and the Victoria Concert Hall and Theatre on your left. At the end you come to the point where Raffles is thought to have first landed on the island. Walk downriver to Cavenagh Bridge and cross over to Boat Quay (► 41), where numerous restaurants offer riverside dining.

SINGAPORE SHOPS: PERANAKAN PLACE TO TANGS DEPARTMENT STORE

From Peranakan Place (► 33), opposite Somerset MRT, you will see John Little (Specialists' Shopping Centre) on the left as you walk down Orchard Road. Further down, just after Grange Road, is Ngee Ann City (► 32), a state-of-the-art shopping complex that opened in 1993. On the right, beyond the Heeren, Paragon and Promenade centres, is Lucky Plaza – here bargaining can be quite fierce. Opposite is Wisma Atria, while at the end of this stretch are Tangs and Orchard MRT. All along Orchard Road there are benches for those wanting to enjoy the hustle and bustle at one remove, and ice-cream and fruit-juice stalls for those needing sustenance. Most shops stay open until 9PM.

INFORMATION

Colonial Singapore
Distance 1½ km
Time 30 mins
Start point Raffles Hotel
✚ F6
Ⓜ City Hall MRT
End point Boat Quay
✚ dI–II/E7
Ⓜ Raffles Place MRT

Singapore Shops
Distance 1km
Start Point Peranakan Place
✚ D6
Ⓜ Somerset MRT
End point Orchard MRT
✚ C5
Ⓜ Orchard MRT

ORGANISED SIGHTSEEING

A host of organised tours is available. For a comprehensive list and up-to-date details contact the Singapore Tourist Board (STB). The Singapore Official Guide, which lists most tours, is available free of charge. The Board also publishes *Singapore This Week* and *The Singapore Visitor*, both of which are free. The main STB office is at Raffles City ✉ #02-34 Raffles Hotel Arcade ☎ 1800 334 1335/6 🕐 Daily 8:30–7.

CITY TOURS

Tours are generally half a day or a day in length, by air-conditioned coach. A variety of tours is available, including: individual attractions such as the zoo or Tang Dynasty Village; city and island tours; historical tours focusing on Raffles, the colonial era and World War II; and even shopping and horse-racing trips. For tours going to one sight the cost is usually at least twice the price you would pay as an independent traveller; thematic tours can be better value.

Designed very much with tourists in mind, the Singapore Trolley Bus plies between some of the city's major attractions such as the Botanic Gardens, Orchard Road, Clarke Quay and the colonial centre. It also stops at major hotels and the World Trade Centre. One-day tickets for unlimited travel are available. Buses operate four times daily – 9:45AM, 10:15AM, 2:45PM and 3:15PM – starting at the Botanic Gardens. Tickets from STB, hotels or ☎ 339 6833. Tickets are also sold on the bus. For tours by trishaw contact Trishaw Tours Pte Ltd ☎ 545 6311. Agree the price before starting.

RIVER AND HARBOUR TRIPS

There are a number of trips on offer. Main operators include: Singapore River Cruises and Leisure ☎ 227 6863/336 6119, river trips 9AM–9PM, departing from North Boat Quay (behind Parliament House); Singapore Explorer Pte Ltd ☎ 339 6833, river trips 9AM–10PM, departing from Clarke Quay; and Eastwind Organisation ☎ 533 3432 and WaterTours ☎ 533 9811, harbour trips from Clifford Pier at 10:30AM, 3PM and 6PM.

Sunday trading

Tangs was first established by a door-to-door salesman, C K Tang, in the 1920s. The devoutly Presbyterian family held out from opening the department store on Sundays until 1994, when the recession in retailing and competition from the surrounding shops caused principles to lose out to profit. Many Singaporeans work on Saturday, so Sunday is a favourite day for shopping.

War memorial

The war memorial (✚ F7 ✉ War Memorial Park) commemorates the tens of thousands of civilians who died during the Japanese Occupation. It is known locally as the 'Four Chopsticks', its design symbolising the four cultures of Singapore: Chinese, Malay, Indian and others. A service is held each year on 15 February – the day Singapore fell to the Japanese in 1942.

19

EXCURSIONS

CHANGI CHAPEL & MUSEUM

Located in the grounds of the current prison, the chapel is a reconstruction of the small, open-air structure built by prisoners of war. Some 85,000 civilians, Allied troops and prisoners were all incarcerated here, and the museum exhibits portray the terrible conditions they endured – some for more than three years. Some prisoners managed to record their experiences, none more movingly than W R M Haxworth, whose sketches vividly capture his years in Changi. George Aspinall, then only 17, secretly photographed life in the prison. James Clavell's *King Rat* draws heavily on the author's time in Changi, giving a powerful, and by all accounts, factual description of the war for many in Singapore. Changi Village makes a good place for lunch.

PULAU UBIN

Pulau Ubin is a rural idyll after the concrete and consumerism of Singapore. Bumboats to the island go whenever they are full. On the ride you will pass one or two *kelongs* – houses on stilts – on which a few fishing families live. At the end of the jetty there is an endearingly scruffy little village. Here coffee can be taken and bicycles hired from the old shop houses. Cycling or walking is peaceful as there are few vehicles on the island. Any walk will take you by the sites of old quarries; huge chunks of the island were removed to build Singapore's tower blocks and the causeway linking Singapore Island to Malaysia. Shaded trails through jungle and abandoned rubber plantations offer some respite from the heat and humidity. On the north-eastern tip of the island there is an excellent seafood restaurant, called – rather unimaginatively – Ubin Seafood!

SUNGAI BULOH NATURE RESERVE

This recently opened nature reserve extends over 87ha and is Singapore's only wetland nature reserve. Carefully planned walkways and hides allow you to explore the brackish swamps,

INFORMATION

Changi Chapel & Museum

✉ Upper Changi Road, Changi Village

☎ 743 7885/543 0893

◷ Mon–Sat 10–5. Closed Sun

🚇 MRT to Tanah Merah then bus 2

Pulau Ubin

🚇 MRT to Tanah Merah then bus 2 to Changi Village, then 10-minute bumboat ride from Changi Jetty to Pulau Ubin

Island ferries

mangrove and mudflat habitats and to observe the wildlife; in particular, mudskippers, crabs and many species of birds can be seen. From September to March it is home to migratory birds from as far afield as eastern Siberia. Early morning and evening are the best times for viewing wildlife. There is an exhibition centre with an audio-visual show five times a day at 9AM, 11AM, 1PM, 3PM and 5PM.

Stilt houses and boats on Pulau Ubin

JOHOR BAHRU

Johor Bahru (or JB, as it is popularly known), a Malaysian town just across the causeway from Singapore, is not the most picturesque of towns but it makes a good contrast to Singapore. The Istana Besar (off Jalan Tun Dr Ismail), with its beautiful gardens and newly opened Royal Museum, and the Sultan Abu Bakar Mosque (further along the same road), are worth visiting. Both were built by Sultan Abu Bakar, in 1866 and 1900 respectively. Abu Bakar was greatly enamoured of all things English and the collection of furniture and Victorian chinoiserie is reminiscent of one of Britain's stately homes.

Foodstalls by the station and the hawker centre in the middle of town offer a choice of meals. Money can be changed from dollars to ringgits at banks or moneychangers in JB or in Singapore.

INFORMATON

Sungai Buloh Nature Reserve
- ✉ Off Neo Tiew Crescent
- ☎ 793 7377
- 🕐 Mon–Fri 7:30–7; Sat–Sun 7–7
- 🚌 Woodlands Interchange then TIBS bus 925 or bus 182 to Kranji War Memorial, then bus 925

Johor Bahru Royal Museum
- ✉ Jalan Tun Dr Ismail
- ☎ 02 07 223 0555
- 🕐 Sat–Thu 9–4

WHAT'S ON

FESTIVALS & EVENTS

With such a wealth of cultures represented in Singapore it is not surprising that it is a city which takes its festivals seriously. All the main religions are recognised and, as well as the major festivals which are taken as public holidays, there is a host of smaller celebrations and events throughout the year. Do note that the dates of many festivals and events are linked to the lunar calendar and change their timing from year to year (▶ 80–1).

JANUARY	*New Year* (1 Jan)
	Ponggal
	River Raft Race
	Thaipusam
JANUARY/FEBRUARY	*Ramadan*
	Hari Raya Puasa
FEBRUARY	*Chinese New Year*
	Chingay Procession
APRIL	*Singapore International Film Festival*
MAY	*Vesak Day*
JUNE	*International Dragon Boat Race*
	Singapore Festival of Asian Performing Arts (biennial, odd-numbered years)
JUNE/JULY	*Great Singapore Sale*
AUGUST	*National Day* (9 Aug)
AUGUST/SEPTEMBER	*Festival of the Hungry Ghosts*
SEPTEMBER	*Mooncake Festival*
	Lantern Festival
OCTOBER	*Thimithi*
OCTOBER/NOVEMBER	*Festival of the Nine Emperor Gods*
NOVEMBER	*Diwali*
DECEMBER	*Christmas* (25 Dec)

WHERE TO FIND OUT WHAT'S ON

Cinema and some music and theatre shows can be very popular, particularly at weekends. Tickets are obtainable from ticketing offices. Cinema tickets can generally be booked a couple of days in advance. Details of events, their venues and where to buy tickets can be found in Singapore's daily newspaper, the *Straits Times*; *8 Days*, a commercial magazine, also gives some information. The STB publishes various free sources of information, including the *Singapore Official Guide* and a calendar of events.
Main SISTIC Ticket Outlets Forum, The Shopping Mall, Scotts Shopping Centre, Specialists' Shopping Centre, Raffles City Shopping Centre, Takashimaya Department Store, East Point, Junction 8, Bugis Junction. Bookings ☎ 348 5555.
Main TicketCharge Outlets Centrepoint, Metro Marina, C K Tang, Wisma Atria, Tanglin Mall, The Substation, Century Square, Funan Centre, Great World City. Bookings ☎ 296 2929.

SINGAPORE's
top 25 sights

The sights are shown on the maps on the inside front cover and inside back cover, numbered **1–25** *from west to east across the city*

23

JURONG BIRDPARK

Hundreds of penguins and puffins crowded together on an icy beach is an unexpected sight when you're just a few miles from the Equator. And don't miss a walk around Waterfall Aviary, where lories, bee-eaters and many other tropical and subtropical avian species fly free – well, almost.

HIGHLIGHTS

- Penguin feeding time
- Jungle Jewels
- Pelican Lake
- Monorail trip
- Waterfall Aviary
- World of Darkness
- Crowned pigeons
- Birds of paradise
- Southeast Asian hornbills and South American toucans
- Southeast Asian Birds Aviary

INFORMATION

- ✚ Off map to west
- ✉ 2 Jurong Hill, Singapore 628925
- ☎ 265 0022
- 🕐 Mon–Fri 9–6; Sat–Sun, public hols 8–6
- 🍴 McDonald's, Waterfall Kiosk, PFS Terrace Kiosk
- 🚇 MRT to Boon Lay then SBS bus 194 or 251
- ♿ Good
- 🚻 Moderate
- ↔ Singapore Science Centre (➤ 25), Chinese and Japanese Gardens (➤ 56)
- ❓ Bird shows: Birds of Prey (10AM, 4PM), All Star (11AM, 3PM), Penguin Parade (10:30AM, 3:30PM)

Jurong BirdPark is Asia-Pacific's biggest bird park – a 20ha home to more than 8,000 birds, many from the tropics. Six hundred species, from all over the world, are housed in an interesting range of aviaries and open enclosures.

Close to the entrance are the penguins, a favourite attraction; they can be seen huddled together in their air-conditioned, glass-sided tank, in which an Antarctic habitat is simulated. Most spectacular is the Waterfall Aviary, where more than 1,200 tropical birds fly free within a huge forested enclosure contained beneath high netting and featuring a 30m waterfall. A monorail trip gives a good overview of the park, but it's well worth getting off to see the birds close up. The Southeast Asian Birds Aviary imitates a rainforest habitat, complete with noon-time deluge, and contains over 100 species, including colourful parrots in the new Parrot Paradise enclosure. Jungle Jewels, the latest attraction, is a walk-through aviary devoted to hummingbirds and other South American species.

White-throated kingfisher

SINGAPORE SCIENCE CENTRE

Hundreds of hands-on exhibits excite children, inspire teenagers and enlighten adults. Rated as one of the ten best in the world, the Science Centre really is an enjoyable place to visit, and shows just how much fun learning can be.

The Singapore Science Centre first opened its doors in 1977 and now attracts over a million visitors each year. A great array of exhibits (more than 600) in themed galleries provides a fascinating insight into human achievements in both the physical and life sciences. Many of the exhibits are interactive, and some are supported by talks and films.

Science to hand Visitors are welcomed in the Atrium by a laser light display. Flight simulators in the Aviation Gallery are especially popular, and other exhibits here explain the history of aviation and the technology of flight. Mathemagic proves that maths can be fascinating and fun, while in the Life Sciences Gallery the focus is on people and the environment. The Discovery Centre aims to stimulate the imagination of younger children, and the Ecogarden is a great inspiration to budding horticulturalists, with its mini orchard, hydroponic farm and medicinal garden. The Hall of Information Technology, opened in 1998, explains the vital role of communications in today's world.

Omni Theatre Next to the Science Centre is the Omni Theatre, which houses a planetarium and an OMNIMAX screening three-dimensional films. This five-storey-high, 23m hemispherical screen has state-of-the-art projection and audio equipment that provides unique views of the universe with startling special effects.

HIGHLIGHTS

- Atrium laser show
- Aviation Gallery
- Discovery Centre
- Hall of Information Technology
- Ecogarden
- Life Sciences Gallery
- Physical Sciences Gallery
- Planetarium
- Omni Theatre

INFORMATION

- ➕ Off map to west
- ✉ 15 Science Centre Road, Singapore 609081
- ☎ 560 3316
- 🕐 SSC: Tue–Sun, public hols 10–6. Omni Theatre: Tue–Sun, public hols 10–9
- 🍴 Café in SSC, fast food in Omni Theatre
- Ⓜ Jurong East MRT then 500m walk (turn left from station, along Block 135) or bus 335
- 🚌 66, 178, 198 direct; 51, 78, 197 to Jurong East Interchange then 335 or walk
- ♿ Good (space for 10 wheelchairs in Omni Theatre)
- 💲 Moderate
- ↔ Jurong BirdPark (➤ 24), Chinese and Japanese Gardens (➤ 56)
- ❓ Planetarium Star Seekers show 10AM, 5PM; OMNIMAX shows 11AM, noon, 1PM, 3PM, 7PM and 8PM

3

BUKIT TIMAH NATURE RESERVE

HIGHLIGHTS

- Winding forest trails
- Rainforest trees
- Strangling figs
- Pitcher plants
- Ferns
- Colourful fungi
- Macaques
- Tree shrews
- Giant ants
- The view
- Mountain-biking trail

INFORMATION

- ✚ Off map to north-west
- ✉ 177 Hindhede Drive, Singapore 589333
- ☎ 468 5736
- 🕐 8:30–6
- 🍴 Visitors' centre vending machine
- Ⓡ MRT to Newton then SBS bus 171 or TIBS 182
- 🚌 5, 67, 170, 171, 172, 181, 184
- ♿ None
- 💲 Free
- ❓ Visitors' centre display and bookshop

The sticky but exhilarating walk up Singapore's highest peak offers a glimpse of majestic tropical rainforest. The 164ha of Bukit Timah hill are one of the few places in Singapore where Nature is allowed to exercise control, unhindered by human interference.

The last remaining area of primary tropical rainforest in Singapore covers 164ha of Bukit Timah hill, at 163m the island's highest point. The forest covering this area has never been logged and, apart from three quarries on its borders, is virgin forest, unchanged for millions of years.

Flora and fauna Trails start from the visitors' centre, allowing you to explore the reserve's fauna and flora. The highlights include splendid dipterocarps – a family of trees, almost all of which were originally only found in Malaysia – some more than 30m tall. Lianas and rattans trail and twist though the forest and strangling figs can be found. The latter are so called because they start life high in the crown of trees and grow aerial roots down to the ground, gradually encircling the host tree; deprived of sunlight at its top and soil nutrients at its base, the tree eventually dies. Smaller epiphytes, with very appropriate names such as bird's-nest fern and staghorn fern, emerge from trunks and branches looking like unkempt bushes.

The animal life is more difficult to spot, except for the marauding macaques, which gather at the base of the reserve and menace for a fight if you get too close – so don't! An early morning visit is best as there is the greatest chance of sighting some of the rarer wildlife. Animals to see include squirrels, lizards and birds such as the greater racket-tailed drongo.

MANDAI ORCHID GARDENS

Rarely, it seems, can nature be improved upon, but some of the orchid hybrids on display at these Gardens are stunning – especially **Vanda 'Mandai Glow'**, *with its beautiful blend of peach and pale orange shades.*

History Orchids have been grown on this site since 1951, when the land was leased by a couple of enthusiasts, John Laycock and Lee Kim Hong, who began growing them. It wasn't until 1956 that it turned into a commercial venture. Following the death of John Laycock, his adopted daughter, Amy Ede, has managed the garden. Now in her seventies, she still goes to the garden each day. The area has increased over the years to 4ha, and today the gardens are the largest on the island, and millions of sprays of orchids are exported all over the world each year.

Mandai Orchid Gardens

The orchids The gardens, running up a slope, are covered in stands of orchids, some native, some introduced, and many hybrids that have been the making of the Singapore orchid industry. Despite the vast array of species on display, amazingly all orchids have the same shape – three sepals and three petals, one of which is known as the 'lip' and which is a completely different shape to the rest. The deep pink and white flowers of *Vanda* 'Miss Joaquim', Singapore's national flower, can be seen in abundance, as can many other varieties, including delicate slipper orchids and fantastic moth orchids. An hour's stroll round the gardens, which, apart from orchids galore, also contain a landscaped water garden, makes a gentle start to the day.

HIGHLIGHTS

- Early morning fragrance
- Black orchid
- Tiger orchid
- *Oncidium* 'Golden Shower'
- Torch ginger
- Jade vine
- Risis jewellery, using gold-dipped orchids

INFORMATION

- ➕ Off map to north-west
- ✉ Mandai Lake Road, Singapore 729827
- ☎ 269 1036
- 🕐 8:30–5:30
- 🍴 Vending machine
- Ⓜ MRT to Ang Mo Kio then SBS bus 138
- 🚌 SBS bus 171 to Mandai Road then cross road for 138, or TIBS 927
- ♿ None
- 💷 Cheap
- ↔ Singapore Zoo (➤ 28)
- ❓ Boxed orchids can be sent abroad – details in shop

5

SINGAPORE ZOO

HIGHLIGHTS

- 'Open enclosures'
- Tigers
- Pygmy hippos
- Primate islands
- Air-conditioned shelters
- Treetops Trail
- Komodo dragons
- Children's World
- Night Safari
- Bearded pigs (Night Safari)

INFORMATION

- Off map to north-west
- Mandai Lake Road, Singapore 729826
- 269 3411. Recorded information: 269 3412
- 8:30–6
- Restaurants. Night Safari: entrance restaurant
- MRT to Ang Mo Kio then SBS bus 138, or MRT to Choa Chu Kang then TIBS 927
- SBS bus 171 to Mandai Road then cross road and take 138
- Good
- Moderate
- Mandai Orchid Gardens (➤ 27)
- Animal shows: breakfast/tea with an orang-utan (9AM, 4PM), primate/reptile show (10:30AM, 2:30PM), elephant/sea lion show (11:30AM, 3:30PM), Animal Friends (1:15PM, plus 4:30PM Sun and public hols). Night Safari – walk or tram ride (7:30PM–midnight)

The zoo's new Treetops Trail, a wooden walkway 6m off the ground, lets you join siamangs (gibbons) and a troop of cheeky red langurs for a monkey's-eye view of a simulated rainforest. It is captivating to watch the endearing langurs as they feed, groom and play with one another.

History Singapore's zoo is acclaimed as one of the finest in the world. It is also one of the youngest – its humble beginnings can be traced back to the 1960s when British Forces families pulled out of Singapore and left a ragbag of pets behind. The zoo was officially opened in 1973 and now has nearly 200 species, some endangered and rare, such as tigers, orang-utans, Komodo dragons and golden lion tamarins.

Animals on show It's an 'open zoo', providing animals with living conditions as close to those of the wild as is feasible – the inmates are contained within mini-habitats bounded by 'natural' moats, trenches and rock walls. Over 2,000 animals are on show, none more popular than the orang-utan, with whom you can have breakfast or tea. The zoo places great emphasis on shows, and there is a wide range to entertain those not content with viewing elephants, chimpanzees, sea lions and the like doing what comes more naturally. Polar bears, otters and pygmy hippos can be seen close up from underwater viewing areas, while the islands created for the different primates allow clear viewing of these hydrophobic creatures. Treetops Trail, the zoo's latest development, is an elevated walkway through simulated rainforest.

Night Safari is a 40ha park next to the zoo where you can walk or ride to see the creatures of the night. The zoo's Children's World offers hands-on experience of sheep and llamas.

6

HAW PAR VILLA (TIGER BALM GARDENS)

This is a cross between Disneyland and Madame Tussaud's, but based on Chinese myth and legend and real-life crimes in old Singapore. Many consider it one of the worst examples of theme-park kitsch – which makes it worth a look in itself.

History In the early 1900s Aw Chu Kin devised the famous panacea Tiger Balm which made the fortune of his sons, Boon Haw (meaning tiger) and Boon Par (leopard), who marketed the potion. In 1937 they built a private residence on this site, 10km west of the city centre. The grounds, with their garish and grotesque statues, were opened to the public after World War II, and became known as the Tiger Balm Gardens. In the 1980s the gardens were sold and rebuilt at a cost of S$85 million, reopening as the Haw Par Villa Dragon World in 1990.

What to see More than a thousand statues portray famous local crimes and 5,000 years of Chinese legend, and show a thoroughly just world in which the bad are caught and punished in a way that fits the crime. The Tales of China boat ride courses through the belly of a 60m-long dragon, where the Ten Courts of Hell show scenes of disturbing brutality complete

with screams. Larger-than-life models and animated puppets bring ancient tales to life. Live performances at the park include a lion dance and the flying stilts acrobats.

Scene from the Ten Courts of Hell

HIGHLIGHTS

- Lion dance
- Stilt acrobats
- Journey to the West
- Laughing Buddha
- Nine Dragons
- Arbisan Plaza
- Ten Courts of Hell
- Tragedy of Lady White Snake
- Wrath of the Water Gods

INFORMATION

- ✚ Off map to west
- ✉ 262 Pasir Panjang Road, Singapore 118628
- ☎ 774 0300
- ◷ Daily 9–6
- 🍴 Fast food
- Ⓡ Buona Vista MRT then bus 200; Clementi MRT then bus 10
- 🚌 10, 30, 51, 143, 200
- ♿ Few
- 🎫 Moderate
- ↔ Mount Faber Park (➤ 56)
- ❓ Lion dance daily 10:30AM, 12:30PM and 3:30PM, plus Sat–Sun 2:45PM

7

BOTANIC GARDENS

INFORMATION

- ➕ A5
- ✉ Junction of Cluny and
  Holland roads, Singapore
  259569
- ☎ 474 1165
- 🕐 Daily 5AM–midnight
- 🍴 Visitor centre restaurant and
  café; vending machine;
  small hawker centre outside
  main gates
- 🚇 MRT to Orchard then SBS
  bus 7, 106, 123 or 174
- 🚌 As above, plus 75, 105
- ♿ Good
- 🎫 Free
- ↔ Orchard Road (➤ 70–1)
- ❓ Occasional outdoor concerts;
  trail leaflets are available
  from the visitor centre

'One of the first things that strikes a visitor is the richness and variety of the tints of the foliage…indeed, the number of different kinds is very large in comparison with that of a more temperate region.' – H N Ridley, Director of the Botanic Gardens, late 19th century.

History Singapore's botanic gardens are a haven of tranquillity, only a few minutes from the clamour of Orchard Road. Covering 52ha, these gardens contain half a million species, with a variety of landscapes, from rolling lawns to orchid gardens and tropical jungle. Raffles established botanical gardens at the base of Government Hill (Fort Canning) in 1822, and the collection was moved to its present site in 1859. Over the decades it has been enlarged and landscaped.

What to see One of the gardens' early directors, Henry Ridley, propagated the first rubber trees in Asia in 1877, from which plantations throughout Malaysia and Indonesia were originally established. Descendants of those first trees, native to Brazil, can still be found today in the gardens. There is, of course, an extensive orchid collection and also many members of the diverse and useful palm family, such as coconut, sago and lontar.

Research and commercial work continues and in the 1960s the gardens supplied many of the seedlings for roadsides and parks all over the island as Singapore 'went green'. The gardens are popular with locals, who jog and picnic and attend the open-air concerts given frequently in Palm Valley. Other attractions include a visitor centre, a cool house for high-altitude orchids, spice gardens and an eco-lake.

8

SENTOSA ISLAND

Even in clean and tidy Singapore the perfect order of Sentosa Island is quite incredible. You will either love or hate the wholesome family package of attractions, but give it a day and you will probably enjoy making up your mind!

This holiday resort, a former pirate lair and later British military base, now attracts over 4 million visitors a year. Sentosa can be reached across a causeway or by a cable car which runs 1.8km from the 116m-high Mount Faber (station at the World Trade Centre).

For the active Rent a canoe or windsurfer, play a round on the Serapong Golf Course (weekdays only), follow the well-signed walks and cycle routes, or relax on 3.2km of beaches.

Adventure Watch a volcano erupt, every half-hour in VolcanoLand; visit Lost Civilization, Asian Village or Fantasy Island, which offers 13 different water rides and 32 slides. See over 350 tropical marine species at Underwater World (feeding times 11:30, 4:30), insects galore at Insect Kingdom and more than 2,500 lepidoptera at Butterfly Park. Waxworks and audio-visuals tell the city's history in Images of Singapore; after this, the Maritime Museum is agreeably low-tech. Visit in the evening for laser and fountain shows, as well as the spotlit Enchanted Grove gnome garden!

Butterfly Park

HIGHLIGHTS

- Cable-car ride
- Underwater World
- Images of Singapore
- Butterfly Park/Insect Kingdom Museum
- Fantasy Island
- VolcanoLand
- Cinemania

INFORMATION

- ✚ Off map to south
- ✉ Sentosa Island, Singapore 099981
- ☎ Sentosa Information Centre: 275 0388. Sentosa Golf Club: 275 0022
- ◷ Mon–Thu 7:30AM–11PM; Fri–Sun, public hols 7:30AM–midnight
- 🍴 Cafés and restaurants islandwide
- 🚠 Cable car from World Trade Centre (WTC – see below) and Mount Faber
- 🚌 To reach WTC (Telok Blangah Road): 10, 30, 61, 65, 84, 93, 97, 100, 131, 143, 145, 166, 176, 855. To reach Sentosa direct: bus A from WTC bus terminal, bus C from Tiong Bahru MRT station, bus E from Orchard Road. Last bus from Sentosa: Mon–Thu 10:30PM; Fri, Sun, public hols 12:30AM
- 🚢 From WTC ferry terminal
- ♿ Few
- 💲 Expensive. Most attractions additional to admission fee; free transport on Sentosa
- ↔ Mount Faber Park (➤ 56)

31

9

NGEE ANN CITY

Ngee Ann City launched itself upon Singapore's nation of shoppers with a 'soft opening', the latest marketing ploy. There was no grand, glitzy opening, rather a trickle of observant passers-by. Of course, it was only a matter of days before the trickle became a flood.

HIGHLIGHTS

- 100 specialist stores
- Harrods
- Tang's Studio
- Food Village
- Maruzen Bookstore
- *Sushi* in the basement
- Sparks Disco
- Exclusive designer names
- Cashmir restaurant
- Virtual Mall

INFORMATION

- C6
- 391 Orchard Road, Singapore 238872
- 736 4741
- 10–9:30. Fourth-floor restaurants: 10AM–11PM
- Restaurants, food courts, supermarket
- Orchard MRT
- 7, 14, 16, 65, 106, 111, 123
- Good
- Free
- Peranakan Place Museum (▶ 33)
- Post office, with overseas delivery; customer service centre

Ngee Ann City is a recent addition to the already mesmerising choice of shopping centres to be found along Orchard Road. This huge complex quickly came to be known as 'Takashimaya', after the owning company, rather than by the name of the building as is usual in Singapore. As one might expect from the name, the most frequent overseas visitors to the mall are from Japan. The plethora of top-of-the-line brand-name stores such as Chanel, Cartier and Tiffany and Co, in addition to the up-market anchor store, Takashimaya, is a great draw.

A wide choice As a break from shopping, customers can watch the free events (of variable quality) staged downstairs in the large basement hall called Takashimaya Square, which is a popular gathering place for one and all. Children can run across a huge world map that covers the floor or watch the 24-screen high-definition television. For the shop- and workaholics of Singapore it is especially popular at weekends and in the evenings, because supplementing the wide choice of merchandise are many other services – all under one roof: a post office, banks, restaurants, food courts, a supermarket, a gym (private) and, that essential ingredient for every successful shopping centre, an underground car park. Visitors will also find the post office on the fourth floor and a customer service centre on the second floor.

PERANAKAN PLACE MUSEUM

The beaded embroidery on show in the museum is exquisite: slippers, knee pads, wall decorations and many other personal and household items, painstakingly decorated, were part of a bride's trousseau.

Peranakan Place Museum The museum, on Orchard Road at the base of Emerald Hill, re-creates a turn-of-the-century Peranakan (Straits Chinese) house. Many of the Straits-born Chinese came from Malacca and married Malays. Many were wealthy and developed close contacts with Europeans, and a distinctive culture formed, known as Peranakan, in which Chinese, Malay and European influences were evident in the clothes, architecture, furnishings and food (*nonya*). The museum is filled with the highly ornate objects favoured by the Peranakans. Chilli Buddy's, just in front of the museum, serves authentic Asian food.

Emerald Hill Just off Orchard Road is Emerald Hill, one of the first areas to be restored by the Urban Redevelopment Authority in the 1980s. Although geared very much to the tourist trade, the street is worth a visit. The area was a small nutmeg plantation in the 1820s and the houses you see today were built only between 1900 and 1930. Many of the old Chinese shop houses have been restored, the garish colours being quite authentic. Those at the bottom of the hill have been converted into boutiques, restaurants and wine bars, while some of those at the top are still used as residences. Look out for some of the interesting architectural details and features such as mirrors – installed to deflect evil spirits.

HIGHLIGHTS

- Carved vents
- Animal motifs symbolising good fortune
- Carved *pintu pagar* – half doors
- Chinese timber signs
- Beaded embroidery
- Bridal bed
- Numbers 63 and 65 Emerald Hill

INFORMATION

- ✚ D6
- ✉ 180 Orchard Road, Singapore 238846
- ☎ 732 6966
- ◷ Mon–Fri 10:30–3
- ▣ Somerset MRT
- ▤ 7, 14, 16, 65, 92, 106, 111, 123, 124, 143, 167, 171, 174, 182, 190, 390, 952
- ♿ Few
- ▣ Moderate
- ↔ Ngee Ann City (➤ 32)
- ❓ Tours available on request

Peranakan Place

11

CHINATOWN

One of the best times to visit Chinatown is just before Chinese New Year, when the crowded streets throb and colourful stalls sell everything from waxed ducks to hong bao *(red packets for giving money as presents). Chinese* wayang *(opera) and lion dances add to the spectacle.*

Singapore's Chinatown is the square kilometre of streets leading off South Bridge Road between Maxwell Road and the Singapore River. Recently, conservation has replaced redevelopment, and though an improvement, the often rather cosmetic results and years of unsympathetic infilling mean that there are now very few streets with the authentic atmosphere and activities of old Chinatown.

What to see Erskine Road and Ann Siang Hill exhibit some of the best efforts of preservation. Temple, Pagoda and Trengganu streets have some traditional shop houses and coffee-shops. People's Park Complex, on Eu Tong Sen Street, offers a wide range of goods, some very local in character – try bargaining here. At 14B Trengganu Street is the Chinaman Scholar's Gallery (➤ 54). East of South Bridge Road, along Lor Telok and Circular Road, there are some examples of nicely decaying shop houses that have yet to feel the conservationist's hand. Telok Ayer Street, again much renovated, is also worth a visit. Thian Hock Keng, currently undergoing major restoration (it reopens in May 2000), is the city's oldest and most beautiful Chinese temple. Far East Square includes Fuk Tak Ch'i, a former temple that now houses a museum dedicated to the story of Singapore's early Chinese immigrants.

12

CLARKE QUAY & RIVERSIDE POINT

You may not be convinced that Clarke Quay lives up to the advertising claims stating that it is Singapore's answer to London's Covent Garden and San Francisco's Fisherman's Wharf, but it's a lively spot none the less.

History Clarke Quay is one of Singapore's most ambitious heritage restoration schemes. Originally a riverside area of old wharves and warehouses, destined for refurbishment, the story goes that the developers got carried away and bulldozed the site before they could be stopped. Maybe re-creating was an easier option than restoring? Whatever, Clarke Quay was opened in 1993, at a cost of S$250 million. The riverfront and streets leading up to River Valley Road have been filled with Disney-style godowns (warehouses), trading posts and shop houses, and colourful junks have been moored in the river.

Shopping and eating The entire area is given over to shops – selling everything from pottery, leather goods and ground coffee to wooden clogs, batik prints and Chinese medicines – and eateries, with alfresco dining a popular option, as at Boat Quay a little further downriver (▶ 41). A year-round carnival atmosphere is attempted with street stalls, stilt walkers and a bandstand complete with entertainment, which is unfortunately usually high on noise but low on quality. For those visitors seeking authentic architecture and artisans' workshops, Clarke Quay is not the place, but for good food, a little local colour and a trip down the river it makes for an interesting evening. If you cross the Read or Ord bridges to the opposite bank you'll find a new development; this is Riverside Point, which boasts a good cinema and the Brewerkz microbrewery.

HIGHLIGHTS

- Riverfront walk
- Street stalls
- Bandstand
- River trip
- Coffee Connection
- J P Bastiani's Mediterranean restaurant
- Thanying Thai restaurant
- Key Largo oyster bar
- Bukhara
- Yunnan Kitchen
- River House
- The Cannery
- Brewerkz

INFORMATION

- b1/E7
- 3 River Valley Road, Singapore 179024
- 433 0152
- Numerous
- Raffles Place MRT
- SBS bus 54 from Scotts Road; 32, 195 from City Hall MRT
- Few
- Free
- Sri Mariamman Temple (▶ 36), Fort Canning Park (▶ 37), Singapore History Museum (▶ 39)
- *Wayang* (Chinese opera) at Gas Lamp Square on Wed and Fri evenings

13

SRI MARIAMMAN TEMPLE

HIGHLIGHTS

- Gopuram
- Thimithi
- Door bells
- Main doors
- Principal hall
- Cows
- Ceiling frescoes
- Shrines

INFORMATION

- bII/E8
- 244 South Bridge Road, Singapore 058793
- 223 4064
- 6–noon, 4–9
- Vending machine outside temple door
- Tanjong Pagar MRT
- SBS bus 61, 103, 166, 197 from City Hall MRT
- None
- Free
- Chinatown (➤ 34)

A devotee burns incense in Sri Mariamman Temple

The cow has always been venerated by Hindus – 'the giver of plenty', as Gandhi wrote. Here, life-size sculptures adorn the temple walls, keeping a watchful eye on the comings and goings in the surrounding streets.

History This building is Singapore's oldest Hindu temple. It is rather surprising to find it here – in the middle of Chinatown – but there has been a Hindu temple on the site since at least 1827. Nariana Pillai, who is thought to have been Singapore's first Indian immigrant, became a successful trader and leader of the Hindu community and erected the first temple in the 1820s. The first wood and *attap* (nipa-palm leaves) structure was replaced by a brick one in 1843, later restored and extended.

What to see The magnificent *gopuram* (ornamental gateway) was erected only in 1903. It is in the southern Indian Tamil style; craftsmen from India were brought to Singapore to build it. The *gopuram*, ceilings and shrines present a riot of colours and shapes. The temple is dedicated to the goddess Mariamman, who has powers to cure epidemics such as cholera and

smallpox. It is still very much a place of worship and visitors should respect this, taking care to remove shoes before entering. The temple is the focus for the annual Thimithi festival, at which devotees walk across a pit of glowing coals to honour the goddess Draupathi.

Fort Canning Park

This area, known during the last century as Government Hill, is an historic high point – quite literally. From 14th-century gold finds to Raffles' house and a late 19th-century fort, the evidence shows that this hill has witnessed many changes in the last 600 years.

Historic hill When Raffles landed in Singapore this hill was known by its Malay name of Bukit Larangan, meaning 'Forbidden Hill', for it was here that the Malay kings were buried. A Muslim shrine, Keramat Iskandar Shah, was also found on the site, as was Javanese gold of the 14th century, indicating the wide-reaching influence of Java at that time. With a commanding view of the harbour and the growing settlement, it was a prime location and was quickly chosen for Government House (the governor's residence). Its slopes were given over to Raffles' experimental garden with its economically useful plants, particularly spices.

Transformations The house was demolished in the mid-19th century and a fort built, named for Viscount Canning. The fort, too, was demolished, in 1907, to make way for a reservoir; all that is left today is the Gothic gateway. On the eastern side of the hill are remnants of an old Christian cemetery. The government offices at the top (built in 1926) house the Fort Canning Centre, and now accommodate a professional dance troupe, exhibition space and a theatre. You can also visit a restored World War II bunker. A spice garden on the south-east slopes re-creates Raffles' early garden.

HIGHLIGHTS

- Christian cemetery
- Keramat Iskandar Shah
- Fort's Gothic gateway
- Five ASEAN sculptures
- Spice garden
- *Bougainvillaea campa*
- Battle Box (World War II bunker)

INFORMATION

- ✚ E6
- ✉ Off Canning Rise, Singapore
- ☎ 332 1200
- 🕔 24 hours
- 🍴 Kiosk at Battle Box, restaurant at Fort Canning Country Club
- Ⓜ Dhoby Ghaut MRT
- 🚍 7, 14, 16, 32, 97, 103, 124, 131, 166, 167, 171, 174, 190, 195
- ♿ None
- 💷 Free
- ↔ Clarke Quay & Riverside Point (➤ 35), Singapore History Museum (➤ 39)

Fort Canning's gateway

15

ANCIENT CIVILISATIONS MUSEUM

HIGHLIGHTS

- Chinese history timeline
- *Nonya* porcelain
- Red bat motifs
- Buddhist statues
- Literati gallery (Gallery 7)
- Jade collection
- Qing Dynasty porcelain
- Kang tables

INFORMATION

- ✚ E6
- ✉ 39 Armenian Street, Singapore 179939
- ☎ 375 2510
- 🕐 Tue–Sun 9–5:30
- 🍴 Café
- 🚇 City Hall MRT
- 🚌 14, 16, 36, 65, 77, 124, 133, 167, 171, 190
- ♿ None
- 💷 Cheap
- ↔ Fort Canning Park (► 37), Singapore History Museum (► 39)
- ❓ Free guided tours Tue–Fri 11AM, 2PM; Sat–Sun 11AM, 2PM, 3:30PM. Museum shop. Temporary exhibition programme

This gem of a museum provides a great introduction to the wonders of 5,000 years of Chinese civilisation. All periods of Chinese history are explored through art and artefacts, from early city plans to a scholar's study, and from Peranakan beaded knee pads to the most finely carved jade.

History The beautiful old Tao Nan School building, dating from 1910, has been restored to its former glory to house the first phase of the Ancient Civilisations Museum. It is the beginning of an ambitious project that aims to showcase the rich history and cultures of Asia. Here, Chinese history is the focus, while in phase II at Empress Place, which is due to open in 2000, India and the other diverse cultures of Asia will be featured. Once complete, this whole project will present a fascinating and inspiring insight into Asia, its historical development and its rich artistic traditions.

Galleries There are 10 galleries, including ones devoted to religion, architecture, ceramics and furniture. Gallery 3 is a real highlight, showing the all-pervading importance of symbolism in Chinese life. Here, the meanings of commonly seen motifs, such as bats, butterflies, pomegranates and peonies, beautifully executed in a range of media, are explained. Elsewhere, an extensive collection of ceramics dating from neolithic times right up to the present day can be seen, including exquisite imperial porcelain, while Gallery 7 explains the honourable if rarefied life of the literati (imperial scholars). Interactive display screens throughout the museum provide additional information for those with particular interests.

SINGAPORE HISTORY MUSEUM

Don't miss the museum's Javanese gold ear pieces and armlets. These are often cited in Singapore's claim to an ancient, glorious, pre-colonial past.

History This fine example of Colonial architecture began life in 1887 as the Raffles Library and Museum. It was originally intended to be twice the size, but the Colonial Office balked at the expenditure and its extent was reduced. The initial collection comprised 20,000 books and many ethnographic artefacts and natural history specimens from the region. Both the permanent displays and temporary exhibitions explore the trends and developments that have shaped Singapore's rich history.

The exhibits Among the items in the permanent collection are Javanese gold jewellery dating from the 14th century found during excavations at Fort Canning, 20 miniature dioramas depicting significant events in Singapore's history, and hundreds of jade carvings. This cache of jade was given by the Aw family, who made their wealth from Tiger Balm (➤ 29). There is a small gallery – Rumah Baba – devoted to the Peranakan (Straits Chinese) culture, where a number of beautiful pieces of porcelain, inlaid blackwood furniture, beaded embroidery, elaborate silverware and clothing are on display. The Children's Discovery Gallery allows for some interactive, educational amusement. Special exhibitions usually have an Asian focus and are a good supplement to the permanent display. Allow two or three hours to explore the museum's collection.

The museum shops, one situated inside the museum and the other down the road on the corner of Armenian Street, sell interesting and good-quality craft items from the region.

HIGHLIGHTS

- Grand entrance
- Central dome
- Javanese gold
- *Sireh* bowls
- Beaded slippers
- Jade carvings
- Opium pipes
- Farquhar Collection of Natural History Drawings
- Porcelain
- Museum shops

INFORMATION

- ✚ E6
- ✉ 93 Stamford Road, Singapore 178897
- ☎ 375 2510
- ◷ Tue–Sun 9–5:30
- 🍴 Small hawker centre next to the National Library
- Ⓜ Dhoby Ghaut MRT
- 🚌 7, 14, 16, 64, 65, 97, 103, 106, 111, 124, 131, 139, 166, 167, 171, 174, 190, 501
- ♿ None
- 💰 Cheap
- ↔ Fort Canning Park (➤ 37), Raffles Hotel (➤ 44)
- ❓ Guided tours in English Tue–Fri 11AM, 2PM; Sat–Sun 11AM, 2PM, 3PM. Guided tours in Japanese Tue–Fri 10:30AM. Occasional talks and fringe activities held by Friends of the Museum

LITTLE INDIA

HIGHLIGHTS

- Sari shops
- Banana-leaf meals
- Fish-head curry
- Perfumed garlands
- Fortune-tellers
- Temples
- Spice shops
- Street corner checkers (draughts) players
- Gold merchants

Typical ornate detail in Little India

INFORMATION

➕ E5

✉ Serangoon Road, Singapore 219785

🍴 Numerous restaurants and cafés

Ⓜ Bugis MRT

🚌 23, 64, 65, 66, 67, 81, 97, 103, 106, 111, 125, 131, 139, 147

♿ None

🎟 Free

↔ Kampung Glam (➤ 46)

Wandering the side streets of Little India is a rich experience of architectural gems, tempting smells, shops stuffed with colourful cloth and baskets overflowing with garlic and chillies. In these streets, unchanged in decades, sensations of the real India can be snatched.

History Serangoon Road and the surrounding streets are known as 'Little India'. In the mid-19th century, lime pits and brick kilns were set up here and it is thought that these first attracted the Indians in Singapore, who were, for the most part, labourers. The area, with its swampy grasslands, was also good for raising cattle – another traditional occupation of the Indian community.

What to see Today, the district is still overwhelmingly Indian, as the sari-clad women, spice shops, jasmine-garland sellers, Indian temples and restaurants show. Apart from the crowded, colourful streets and the tempting food emporiums, there is also the huge Zhujiao food market at the beginning of Serangoon Road; upstairs you will find both clothes and luggage on sale. Opposite the market and on a little street is Komala Vilas Restaurant. For those in need of lunch or a snack it's a must, serving wonderful *dosai* (savoury pancakes) and *thali* (mixed curries) – all vegetarian. Carry on along the Serangoon Road and you will come to the Sri Veeramakaliamman Temple, which is dedicated to the ferocious goddess Kali. Further on still is the Sri Srinivasa Perumal Temple with its magnificent *gopuram*, a 1979 addition. Take a detour to Race Course Road for a range of restaurants, notably those offering fish-head curry.

BOAT QUAY

The bundles of rattan and sacks of rice have long disappeared, as have the coolies and boatmen, but the sweep of shop houses, the thronging crowds and the odd tour operator's bumboat give an inkling of the river's former life and the fortunes still being made on it.

After decades as a sleepy backwater, Boat Quay has sprung back into life. For a century after the founding of Singapore, it was 'a place of ceaseless activity' – Bu Ye Tian, as the Chinese used to call it – with bumboats and sampans ferrying their cargoes of rubber and rice, sago and spices, cotton and rattan, back and forth to ships at Tanjong Pagar Docks. The riverbank was lined with shop houses serving as trading offices and godowns for storage and sorting. Behind was Commercial Square (now Raffles Place), where the large international shipping and trading companies had their commercial offices.

New role With the opening of the city's large container port facilities the *raison d'être* for Boat Quay was lost, the bumboats were cleared and the area was left to a few traders and mechanics who continued to scratch a living there. Then, in the late 1980s, the area was designated a conservation area and life was restored to the riverbank. The shop houses were renovated and a riverside walkway built. Most of the shop houses are now bars and restaurants, and the riverside is awash with tables and chairs for alfresco dining. It's a picturesque, though busy stretch and offers pleasant dining with views across to Raffles' first landing site, Empress Place, and the impressive multi-storey towers of the new Singapore.

HIGHLIGHTS

- Views of river
- Contrasts – shop houses and skyscrapers
- Raffles' landing place
- Cavenagh Bridge
- Harry's Quayside café
- House of Sundanese Food
- Our Village
- Kinara Indian restaurant
- Bumboats at night
- Tower Books

INFORMATION

- ✚ bI–II/E7
- ✉ Boat Quay, Singapore
- 🍴 Restaurants and cafés galore
- Ⓜ Raffles Place MRT
- 🚌 70, 75, 80, 82, 97, 100, 130
- ♿ Few
- 🎟 Free
- ↔ Chinatown (➤ 34), Sri Mariamman Temple (➤ 36), Fort Canning Park (➤ 37), Raffles Hotel (➤ 44)
- ❓ River tours

41

19

BISHAN – HDB ESTATE

To get a feel for modern Singapore it's important to see the Singapore that most locals know – where they live, eat, shop and do their washing. You will then catch a glimpse of a Singapore that doesn't feature in the tourist-board posters.

HIGHLIGHTS

- Junction 8
- Multi-screen cinema complex
- Local coffee-shops
- Local market stalls
- Steamboat meals
- Raffles Institution

INFORMATION

- ✚ Off map to north
- ✉ Bishan Central, Singapore
- 🍴 Numerous coffee-shops, hawker centres and fast-food outlets
- Ⓜ Bishan MRT
- 🚌 13, 53, 54, 55, 56, 156
- ♿ Few
- ✋ Free

At a Bishan hawker centre

History The vast majority of Singapore's population lives in Housing Development Board apartments (HDBs). These government-built blocks – hundreds constructed in one area – form small new towns. Bishan is one of the more recent additions to the list of estates. As with most HDB areas, Bishan has its own MRT station, around which a vast shopping and entertainment complex, called Junction 8, has been built. Wander round the central area close to the MRT station, but also walk up Bishan Road (turn right in front of the MRT) and left into Street 22. You'll come upon one of the many smaller satellite community areas, complete with its own shops and hawker centre at the base of the residential blocks.

Bishan is also home to the prestigious Raffles Institution, the school Raffles founded, now at its third site. On the outskirts of Bishan, at Bright Hill Drive, is Phor Kark See, a huge Buddhist temple complex. The best times to visit Bishan are in the early morning, when housewives are out doing their shopping, or early evening, when families get together to shop and have their evening meal at the hawker centre. Try a steamboat (Chinese fondue) meal yourself, either at a hawker centre or at 3rd Mini Steamboat Delight ✉ 9 Bishan Place, #04-01G ☎ 353 6498 near Bishan bus interchange behind the main shopping complex – just choose the items you want and pop them into the boiling stock to cook – delicious!

THE PADANG

The word padang *is Malay for 'plain', and that is just what this is. Although unrelieved by trees or hills, these few hectares offer a good breathing space and act as a focal point for the colonial buildings grouped around.*

Once the Padang faced on to the sea directly, but land reclamation in Marina Bay has long since changed its outlook. Set aside by Raffles, the Padang has retained its use as a recreational space. Cricket and rugby are played – in season, of course – and while non-members may not venture into the clubs at either end of the Padang, they can stand and watch the games. St Andrew's Cathedral, behind the Padang, was built in 1861 with Indian convict labour. The City Hall, facing the Padang, has witnessed a number of historic events: the herding of Europeans on to the Padang on the morning of Japanese occupation, the formal surrender of the Japanese in 1945 on its steps and, since 1965, many National Day rallies.

At the southern end is the Cricket Club, with a commanding view of the Padang. The collection of government buildings includes the Attorney-General's Chambers (looking like a small opera house), Parliament House and the Victoria Theatre and Concert Hall buildings. Turning back down Connaught Drive and Esplanade Park, you will see the outline of Suntec City – a huge conference and exhibition centre and a group of hotels built on reclaimed land, together with Marina Square Shopping Centre. At the northern end of the Padang is the Recreation Club, originally built in 1885 for Eurasians, who were excluded from the Cricket Club at the opposite end of the Padang.

HIGHLIGHTS

- City Hall steps
- Singapore Cricket Club
- Cricket matches
- Attorney-General's House
- Victoria Theatre portico
- Concert Hall tea-room
- Esplanade Walk
- War Memorial Park
- St Andrew's Cathedral

INFORMATION

- F7
- St Andrew's Road, Singapore 178957
- City Hall MRT
- 10, 70, 75, 82, 97, 100, 107, 125, 130, 131, 167, 196
- None
- Free
- Fort Canning Park (➤ 37), Boat Quay (➤ 41), Raffles Hotel (➤ 44)

Westin Stamford Hotel and Raffles City

43

21

RAFFLES HOTEL

INFORMATION

- ✚ F6
- ✉ 1 Beach Road, Singapore 189673
- ☎ 337 1886
- 🍽 Café and restaurant
- Ⓜ City Hall MRT
- 🚌 56, 82, 100, 107, 125
- ♿ Good
- ↔ Fort Canning Park (➤ 37), Boat Quay (➤ 41), the Padang (➤ 43)
- ❓ Free museum (🕐 10–9); shopping arcade complete with hotel shop; STB office (✉ #02-34 Raffles Hotel Arcade)

Those who are able to compare say the renovators have tried a little too hard – the Long Bar, for instance, has been repositioned to allow for a two-storey bar to cater for the influx of visitors, and there is not an inch of flaking plaster to be seen – but Raffles Hotel is still the 'Grand Old Lady of the East'.

The hotel Say 'Raffles' and you conjure up an image of the very epitome of colonial style and service. Established by the Sarkies brothers in 1887, the hotel served the traders and travellers who, after the opening of the Suez Canal in 1869, were visiting the bustling commercial hub of Singapore in growing numbers. Within a decade of opening, the original 10-room bungalow had been expanded and two-storey wings added. The main building (the front) was opened in 1899. Over the years the hotel has built up a reputation for fine service and food, and has also gained renown internationally as a traveller's paradise, with its unique blend of classical architecture and tropical garden setting.

The people Through the years guests have included Rudyard Kipling, Somerset Maugham, Noël Coward, Elizabeth Taylor and Michael Jackson. A museum dedicated to Raffles memorabilia is a must for those who are filled with nostalgia for the 'golden age of travel'.

Sikh doorman at Raffles

BUGIS STREET

The new Bugis Village, a pale imitation of the original Bugis Street, offers a sanitised version of the street life found in some of Asia's other cities. The clubs and market stalls are back, but goods are no longer fakes and the pushy touts are trapping tourists only for the open-air restaurants and bars.

Yesterday Bugis Street was the sin centre of old Singapore, the haunt of prostitutes and transvestites. Such activities were disapproved of by the Singaporean authorities, and the street was totally demolished in 1980 to make way for the Bugis MRT station. Remembered with affection and sought for in vain by tourists, however, it was rebuilt in 1991, 137m from its original site. Six blocks of Chinese shop houses and some of the more celebrated original buildings were re-created.

Today The night market is open until late. Luxury goods tend to be sold near Victoria Street, crafts and curios further down, and fruit and vegetables near Albert Street. Around the edge of the Village are fast-food outlets, shops selling fashion clothes, a traditional herbalist and a tea specialist. One of the liveliest attractions is the Boom Boom Room ✉ Albert Street 🕐 Mon–Fri 8:30PM–2AM; Sat–Sun 8:30PM–3AM. It stages two cabaret shows each night and features the 1940s-style Boom Boom Bar, where jazz is played.

Over Bugis MRT station is the 120,000sq m Bugis Junction shopping and office complex, where the re-created old terraces of Hylamon Street are cocooned under a glass roof and now house boutiques and up-market shops.

HIGHLIGHTS

- Boom Boom Bar
- Boom Boom Room
- Boutiques
- Bugis Junction
- Chinese herbalist
- Hylamon Street
- Night market
- Open-air restaurants

INFORMATION

- ✚ F6
- ✉ Bugis Street, Singapore
- ☎ Boom Boom Room: 339 8187
- 🕐 Market: open to midnight. Bars: open to 2 or 3AM
- 🍴 Open-air restaurants, fast-food outlets
- Ⓢ Bugis MRT
- 🚌 2, 5, 7, 12, 32, 61, 62, 63, 84, 130, 160, 197, 520, 851, 960
- ♿ Few (pedestrian precinct)
- 🍽 Moderate bars and food, antiques and crafts
- ↔ Little India (▶ 40), Kampung Glam (▶ 46)
- ❓ Boom Boom Room shows 10PM, 1AM

KAMPUNG GLAM

HIGHLIGHTS

- Bussorah Street
- Gilded dome of Sultan Mosque
- Prayer hall
- Istana Kampung Glam
- *Murtabak*
- *Batik*
- Leather satchels
- Arab Street

INFORMATION

Sultan Mosque

- F6
- 3 Muscat Street, Singapore 198833
- 293 4405
- 9–4
- Numerous coffee-shops
- Bugis MRT
- 2, 32, 51, 61, 63, 84, 133, 145, 197
- None
- Free
- Raffles Hotel (➤ 44), Bugis Street (➤ 45)

Rainbow hues for sale

Another face of Singapore – the domes, minarets and cupolas of Sultan Mosque, glinting in the afternoon sunlight – reminds you that this area of Singapore is very much part of the Islamic world.

History Kampung Glam was set aside in the early days of Singapore as an area for Malays and Arab and Bugis traders. It was here that the sultan of Singapore lived. It is thought that the area was named 'Glam' after the *gelam* tree from which medicinal oil was produced; the area is now part of a designated conservation area. The *istana* (palace), constructed in the 1840s, is located at the top of Sultan Gate and is worth viewing. The surrounding streets are good for finding souk items: basketware, batik, perfume and leather goods. The Muslim coffee-shops serve a tasty range of Indian Muslim dishes such as *murtabak* (curry pancake) and beef *rendang* (cooked in coconut milk).

Sultan Mosque is the main focus of worship for Singapore's Muslim (mainly Malay) community, although there are 80 mosques on the island. There has been a mosque on this site since 1824, when the East India Company made a grant for its construction. The present mosque dates from 1928, and reveals an interesting mixture of Middle Eastern and Moorish influences. Its gilded dome is impressive; unusually, its base is made from bottles. Seen as you walk up Bussorah Street, with its shop houses at the rear, it is a stunning sight. Visitors are welcome outside prayers times, as long as they are well covered – no shorts!

EAST COAST PARK

Two decades of land reclamation have created this beachside playground. Swim or sail; walk, jog or cycle the 10km of tracks between coconut groves and bird sanctuaries; play in high-tech amusement arcades; or laze on white sands with views of Indonesia's Riau Islands and ships in the Singapore Straits.

Singapore's East Coast Park offers a wealth of sporting activities and leisure facilities, with numerous cycle, canoe and deck-chair hire kiosks, as well as the centres listed below (from east to west). It's also a good area to visit in the evenings for local seafood and cooling breezes.

East Coast Sailing Centre A busy rescue boat returns inexperienced hirers of windsurfers and laser dinghies to the East Coast Sailing Centre; lessons are also available. The Urban Management and Development Corporation (UDMC) clubhouse has good leisure facilities and sports equipment for hire.

East Coast Recreation Centre Next to the fun park at the East Coast Recreation Centre are clay tennis courts (open until late evening), and two ten-pin bowling centres and a snooker and billiards hall (open until the early hours). Golf fanatics can practise at the two-tier 150m Parkland for just the cost of the balls. At the Big Splash, water rides delight both adults and children, and in the same complex local bands entertain at the Europa Disco each evening.

Singapore Crocodilarium Around 1,000 crocodiles can be found lurking at the Crocodilarium, where they are farmed. Crocodile-skin products are also showcased here.

HIGHLIGHTS

- Big Splash water rides
- Canoe hire
- East Coast Lagoon Food Rendezvous hawker centre
- East Coast Sailing Centre
- Mastercue snooker and billiards
- Parkland Golf Driving Range
- Tennis Centre
- White-sand beaches

INFORMATION

- H–N6
- East Coast Service Road, Singapore 449880
- ECSC: 449 5118. Regent Bowl: 443 1518. Tennis Centre: 442 5966. Parkland Golf Range: 440 6726. Big Splash: 345 1211. Europa Disco: 447 0869. Crocodilarium: 447 3722. Ponggol Seafood: 448 8511
- UDMC Seafood Centre, Ponggol Seafood Restaurant, various kiosks, fast food at ECRC and Big Splash
- Bedok MRT then bus 401 or bus 31, 197; Eunos MRT then 55, 155; Paya Lebar MRT then 76, 135, and walk
- 16, 31, 55, 76, 135, 155, 196, 197, 853 daily to Marine Parade Road; 401 to East Coast Service Road (Sun)
- Some level paths
- Free; hire charges per hour for sports, etc
- Changi Chapel (➤ 20), Joo Chiat Road (➤ 48)

47

25

JOO CHIAT ROAD

INFORMATION

- L4–5
- Joo Chiat Road, Singapore
- Guan Hoe Soon: 344 2761.
  Katong Antique House:
  345 8544
- Guan Hoe Soon (*nonya*
  food, no 214); Casa
  Bom Vento (no 47);
  Mum's Kitchen (no 314);
  AJ Tandoori's (no 328);
  Lemongrass (899 East
  Coast Road)
- Paya Lebar MRT then walk
- 16, 33
- None
- Free
- East Coast Park (▶ 47)

Wonderful architecture, a fascinating range of old trade businesses by day, and an exciting mix of restaurants of different nationalities and music lounges in the evening make Joo Chiat Road a genuine, unpackaged sample of Singapore life today, and give a fascinating glimpse of former times.

The development of Katong, once a quiet seaside village, was begun after World War I by Chew Joo Chiat. Today, an eclectic mix of colonial villas, Malay bungalows and Peranakan-style terraces remains. Some are preserved, many undergoing renovation, others untouched for decades. The Joo Chiat Complex, at the northern end of Joo Chiat near the new Malay Village Centre, is a bustling locals' shopping complex selling fabrics and household goods at bargain prices.

Opposite Guan Hoe Soon Restaurant (which serves traditional Peranakan *nonya* dishes) is a typical 1920s corner terrace, with an ornate frieze of green dragons on the roof pediment. Along the road are terraces with covered walkways. The second storeys may be pillared verandas (no 113), or have ornate casement windows (nos 370–6). Colourful tilework is a common feature (nos 137–9). Koon Seng Road, to the left, has two facing rows of colourful terraces with courtyard gardens to the front, and extravagant mouldings, tiles and paintwork. Set in dense gardens are Malay-style elevated bungalows (nos 229, 382) with verandas to the front, flanked by staircases. Villas near the southern end (nos 507–9) recall that this was the sea front before land reclamation. Turn left to the Katong Antique House, at no 208, or right into East Coast Road.

SINGAPORE's *best*

MODERN ARCHITECTURE

Going up!

Don't miss the ride in the high-speed lift of the Westin Stamford Hotel — the only way to get to the top of its 73 storeys. A matter of seconds after leaving the ground floor you are deposited 226m in the air.

The Ritz-Carlton Millennia Hotel

See Top 25 Sights for NGEE ANN CITY ➤ 32

THE GATEWAY
The twin towers of this office development – 37 storeys of darkly tinted glass – dominate this part of Beach Road. The structure, with a distinctive gap in the middle, is loosely inspired by traditional Balinese split gates.
✚ F6 ✉ 152 Beach Road 🚇 City Hall MRT 🎫 Free

RITZ-CARLTON MILLENNIA HOTEL
Singapore's newest and most stylish luxury hotel is built on reclaimed land in Marina Bay. The iridescent glass-domed roof of the lobby is a key feature, while the understated grandeur of the interior design provides a relaxing atmosphere.
✚ F7 ✉ 7 Raffles Avenue ☎ 337 8888 🍴 Three restaurants
🚇 Raffles City MRT 🎫 Free

SINGAPORE MARRIOTT
This 33-storey hotel makes an unusual change from most modern buildings, with its fanciful pagoda-style roof. Although it could not be classed as an authentic shape, it makes a very good local landmark.
✚ C5 ✉ 320 Orchard Road ☎ 735 5800 🍴 Numerous restaurants 🚇 Orchard MRT 🎫 Free

SUNTEC CITY

Singapore's new international convention and
exhibition centre is built in line with *feng shui*
principles, alongside towers and with the world's
largest fountain.

🕂 F7 ✉ Raffles Boulevard ☎ 295 2888 🕘 9AM–10PM
🍴 Numerous restaurants 🚇 Raffles City MRT 💵 Free

UOB PLAZA

The 66-storey UOB Plaza building at the bottom of
Boat Quay is impressively out of scale with the small
shop houses along the river. At 280m, it is as high
as Singapore building regulations allow.

🕂 dll/E8 ✉ 80 Raffles Place, UOB Plaza 1 ☎ 533 9898
🍴 Top of the Plaza Cantonese restaurant (🕘 11:30–3, 6–10:30)
🚇 Raffles Place MRT 💵 Free

WESTIN STAMFORD HOTEL

At 226m (with 73 storeys) this is one of the
world's tallest hotels. The Compass Rose Bar
and Restaurant, right at the top, allows fantastic
views over much of the island.

🕂 F7 ✉ 2 Stamford Road, Raffles City ☎ 338 8585
🍴 Many 🚇 City Hall MRT 💵 Free

WHEELOCK PLACE

The stylish glass and stone structure
contains one of the island's many
shopping complexes. The glass
pyramid fronting Orchard Road makes
an unusual addition to the shops and
hotels up and down this busy
thoroughfare.

🕂 C5 ✉ 501 Orchard Road 🕘 10–10
🍴 Cafés
🚇 Orchard MRT
💵 Free

Going underground

The northern loop of Singapore's
state-of-the-art metro system, the
Mass Rapid Transit (MRT), has
recently been completed. An
ambitious five-year project is now
well under way to build the
north-east line, which will link the
World Trade Centre with Punggol.

The 66-storey UOB Plaza

COLONIAL STYLE

Watering holes

Try the Somerset Bar in the Westin Stamford Hotel for evening drinks and live jazz. Alternatively, there is the fabled Long Bar (newly rebuilt) at Raffles, where, amazingly in litter-free Singapore, the tradition is to throw your empty peanut shells on to the floor.

> **See Top 25 Sights for**
> **THE PADANG ➤ 43**
> **RAFFLES HOTEL ➤ 44**

COLONIAL RESIDENCES

A walk along Cluny, Lermit and Nassim roads, between the west end of Orchard Road and the Botanic Gardens, will give glimpses of colonial era residences. These grand 'black and white' mansions come complete with features for making living in the tropical heat as tolerable as possible: enormous blinds, shaded balconies and verandas, and landscaped gardens rich with foliage.

✚ A–B5 ✉ Cluny, Lermit and Nassim roads 🚇 Orchard MRT 🎟 Free

GOODWOOD PARK HOTEL

Clubs were very much part of colonial life as a place for expatriates to meet their fellows. This building, erected in 1900, started life as the Teutonia Club for the German population of Singapore. Although there have been many alterations, the front, with its pretty turrets, has remained unchanged. It was converted into a hotel after World War II.

✚ C5 ✉ 22 Scotts Road ☎ 737 7411 🍴 Numerous restaurants 🚇 Orchard MRT 🎟 Free

POLO CLUB

Although the Polo Club is located a little way out of town, its veranda makes a pleasant place for enjoying a 'sundowner' and dinner as the light fades over the polo field. Non-members are allowed entry to the bar and restaurant.

✚ D2 ✉ 80 Mount Pleasant Road ☎ 256 4530 🕐 8–11 🍴 Restaurant, bar 🚌 54, 130, 132, 156, 166 🎟 Free

RAFFLES HOTEL – BILLIARDS

The sporting institution of billiards was a favourite during the days of the British Empire. The Billiards Room at the Raffles Hotel houses a 100-year-old

Action at the Singapore Polo Club

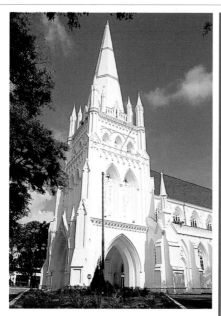

The starkly white, Gothic-style St Andrew's Cathedral

table and serves the famous Singapore sling – a good way to unwind after a hard day's sightseeing.

RAFFLES HOTEL – TIFFIN

Tiffin, meaning a light meal, is a word originally associated with the midday meal colonial officials in India would take; a mixture of English and Asian fare was usually served. A splendid tiffin buffet is available, lunch and dinner, in the Tiffin Room.
➕ F6 ✉ 1 Beach Road ☎ 337 1886 🍴 Numerous restaurants 🚇 City Hall MRT

ST ANDREW'S CATHEDRAL

Completed in 1861, St Andrew's was very much the focus of religious life for the Anglican community during colonial times and is still a popular place of worship. It was built by convict Indian labour and the whiter-than-white exterior is said to have been achieved by the use of Madras *chunan* – a mixture of shell lime, egg white and sugar – often used in India.
➕ E7 ✉ St Andrew's Road ☎ 337 6104 🕐 8–6 🚇 City Hall MRT 🎟 Free

SINGAPORE CRICKET CLUB

This historic building is a very good example of a late Victorian-era sports club, though unfortunately it is not open to the public. However, you can admire the pavilions and verandas from the outside.
➕ E7 ✉ St Andrew's Road 🚇 City Hall MRT 🎟 No admittance to non-members

MUSEUMS & PLACES OF WORSHIP

Dragons

Dragons are a common symbol found in Chinese temples, and represent the opposing forces of *yin* and *yang*. In Thian Hock Keng Temple (➤ 34) they can be seen on the roof ridges and carved on the huge granite pillars near the entrance.

Gold dragon in Thian Hock Keng Temple

> See Top 25 Sights for
> **ANCIENT CIVILISATIONS MUSEUM ➤ 38**
> **SINGAPORE HISTORY MUSEUM ➤ 39**
> **SULTAN MOSQUE, KAMPUNG GLAM ➤ 46**

MUSEUMS

CHINAMAN SCHOLAR'S GALLERY

A small museum in an old shop house in the heart of Chinatown, which re-creates the home of a Chinese scholar of the 1920s and 1930s. Kitchen, bedroom, and living and dining rooms are all laid out with furniture and fittings in keeping with the period. There are a number of interesting exhibits, including classical Chinese musical instruments and embroidery. The Chinese tea ceremony is explained and performed.

✚ bII/E8 ✉ 14B Trengganu Street 🕐 Mon—Sat 9—4 🚇 Outram Park MRT 💷 Cheap

RAFFLES MUSEUM

This is a charming small museum, and was set up when the newly renovated hotel reopened in 1991. Artefacts and memorabilia associated with the hotel were gathered together from its own collection and by advertising. The result is a delightful display of early plans and photographs, personal letters and postcards (some from well-known guests), luggage labels, travel posters and the like.

✚ F6 ✉ Raffles Hotel Arcade ☎ 337 1886 🕐 10—9 🍴 Many near by in Raffles Hotel and Raffles City 🚇 City Hall MRT 💷 Free

SINGAPORE ART MUSEUM

The Singapore Art Museum is housed in a former school, St Joseph's Institution. Among the 400 exhibits on display are many by Singaporean and Southeast Asian artists, with the focus very much on contemporary art.

✚ E6 ✉ 71 Bras Basah Road ☎ 375 2510 🕐 Tue—Sun 9—5:30 🍴 Caf 🚇 City Hall MRT

PLACES OF WORSHIP

ARMENIAN CHURCH

The Armenian Church, the Church of St Gregory the Illuminator, was built in 1835 for the small Armenian community which even at that early date had already been attracted to the growing port of Singapore. It has the distinction of being the oldest surviving Christian church in Singapore, though it is no longer used as a place of worship.

🕂 E7 ⊠ Hill Street ☎ 334 0141 ⏰ 8–8 Ⓜ City Hall MRT 👆 Free

CHETTIAR HINDU TEMPLE

This temple (rebuilt in 1983), the Sri Thandayuthanapani Temple, is also called the Chettiar Hindu Temple because the *chettiars*, money-lenders, financed its original construction in the 1850s. The *gopuram* is a riot of images and colours. An unusual feature is the 48 glass-panel ceiling frieze, brought from India, each panel featuring a deity from the Hindu pantheon.

🕂 D6 ⊠ 15 Tank Road ☎ 737 9393 ⏰ 8–noon, 5:30–8:30 Ⓜ Dhoby Ghaut MRT 👆 Free

Detail of the gopuram of the Chettiar Hindu Temple

NAGORE DURGHA SHRINE

This small mosque, close to Thian Hock Keng Temple, was built around 1820 for the Indian Muslim community by Chulias, southern Indian Muslims from the Coromandel Coast. Painted in green, with tiny minarets and a façade of small archways and delicate plaster grilles, it is a picturesque and beautiful sight.

🕂 cII/E8 ⊠ 140 Telok Ayer Street ☎ 324 0021 ⏰ 10–10 Ⓜ Raffles Place MRT 👆 Free

SRI SRINIVASA PERUMAL TEMPLE

Like many of the Hindu temples in Singapore, this temple has a number of common elements: a *gopuram*, a main worshipping hall and a shrine for the gods. The *gopuram* was built in 1979, funded by a leading Singapore merchant, P Govindasamy Pillai, whose name you may see on one or two of the stores in Little India.

🕂 F4 ⊠ Serangoon Road ☎ 298 5771 ⏰ 6–noon, 6–9 Ⓜ Bugis MRT 👆 Free

Singapore's national flower

The orchid *Vanda 'Miss Joaquim'* – a natural hybrid – is named after Agnes Joaquim, who discovered it one morning in 1893 growing in her garden. She is buried in the small graveyard attached to the Armenian Church.

GARDENS & GREEN SPACES

What's in a name?

The Chinese Garden is full of wonderfully romantically named sites: Cloud-Piercing Pagoda, Courtyard of Early Spring, Moon Inviting Boat and Tiger's Roar Waterfall. With romance in the air, the gardens are extremely popular with young couples as a backdrop for wedding photographs.

> **See Top 25 Sights for**
> **BOTANIC GARDENS ➤ 30**
> **BUKIT TIMAH NATURE RESERVE ➤ 26**
> **FORT CANNING PARK ➤ 37**
> **MANDAI ORCHID GARDENS ➤ 27**

CHINATOWN/TANJONG PAGAR

If you feel like a little tranquillity after the hustle and bustle of Chinatown, find the path (backing Bukit Pasoh and Craig roads) that runs between New Bridge Road, opposite the Pearl Centre, and Tanjong Pagar. Shady trees and handy benches line the route, which takes you past renovated shop houses and a Buddhist temple and brings you out at Tanjong Pagar food centre.

➕ bIII/D8 ✉ Bukit Pasoh and Craig roads

CHINESE AND JAPANESE GARDENS

Chinese and Japanese classical gardens have been created on two islands in Jurong Lake. The Chinese Garden covers 13ha and is dotted with pagodas, pavilions and arched bridges. The main building is based on Beijing's Summer Palace. During the mid-autumn festival the gardens are hung with lanterns. The Japanese Gardens are altogether more serene, and take their inspiration from gardens of the 15th–17th centuries.

➕ Off map to west ✉ Chinese Garden Road ☎ 264 3455
⏰ 9–6:30 🍴 Refreshment kiosks 🚇 Chinese Garden MRT
💲 Moderate

A pagoda in the Chinese Garden

MACRITCHIE RESERVOIR PARK

If you're in need of a little exercise, you can jog, or simply walk, on the shaded paths around the reservoir's edge; for the keenest, special 'exercise areas' have been added at intervals. From the bridge you can watch turtles and carp, and, if it's switched on, see the fountain, which allegedly plays 30 different water-jet patterns. Concerts are sometimes given in the pavilion.

➕ C1 ✉ Lornie Road ⏰ 24 hours
🍴 Food kiosk 🚇 MRT to Newton then bus 104 or 132 💲 Free

MOUNT FABER PARK

Rewarding views of Keppel Harbour, Sentosa Island and, on clear days, some of the Indonesian Riau

Islands can be seen from the top of Mount Faber – a signal station in the 19th century. The park's 73ha have been planted with a variety of trees and shrubs, the bougainvillaea being particularly noticeable. From the top of Mount Faber is a cable car to the World Trade Centre and Sentosa Island.

B9 ✉ Mount Faber Road ⏱ 24 hours 🍴 Café Ⓜ MRT to City Hall then bus 61, 124, 143 or 166 🎟 Free

PASIR RIS PARK

This area contains some of Singapore's last remaining stretches of mangrove swamp, and is now conserved as a bird and nature reserve. Raised boardwalks allow you to walk through this habitat without getting muddy. Look out for fiddler crabs, mudskippers, small-clawed otters and herons. Other birds you might spot include yellow-vented bulbuls, brown-throated sunbirds and collared kingfishers.

Off map to north-east ✉ Off Jalan Loyang Kechil ⏱ 24 hours Ⓜ MRT to Pasir Ris then bus 403 🎟 Free

PULAU UBIN ISLAND ➤ 20

ST JOHN'S ISLAND

This relatively unspoilt island is good for walking and picnicking. People do swim and laze about on the beaches, but conditions – as with most of Singapore's beaches – are not ideal as the island is located in the middle of one of the world's busiest shipping routes. Try to avoid weekends as it can get crowded.

Off map to south ☎ 270 3918 for ferry details 🍴 Café ⛴ Ferry from World Trade Centre (Mon–Sat 10AM, 1:30PM; six sailings on Sun from 9:45AM) 🎟 Ferry tickets moderate

SUNGAI BULOH NATURE RESERVE ➤ 20

St John's Island

Mangroves – unique adaptations

Mangrove plants are adapted to survive in salty, swampy conditions. Some species have 'breathing roots', called pneumatophores, others a tangle of aerial roots. These adaptations allow the plant to take in more oxygen, which helps it eliminate the salt absorbed from the water. You can see mangroves at Sungai Buloh and Pasir Ris reserves.

57

Parascending is just one of the many sports possible in Singapore

OUTDOOR ACTIVITIES

ARCHERY

ARCHERY TRAINING CENTRE
The only centre for archery *aficionados* and anyone wishing to take up the sport. It has a range that allows shooting up to 70m.
✚ D2 ✉ Singapore Polo Club, 80 Mount Pleasant Road ☎ 760 1300 🕐 9–6 🚌 160, 166, 851 💰 Moderate; courses start at S$150 for six lessons

BIKE HIRE

SDK RECREATION
Bike hire available near the East Coast Recreation Centre, and one of many kiosks along the East Coast Parkway cycle track. Lights and some safety equipment also available.
✚ Off map to east ✉ 1000 East Coast Parkway, #01-00 ☎ 445 2969/241 5214 🕐 Sun–Fri 8:30–8; Sat and public hols 9–8 🍽 Cafés and restaurants near by 🚇 Bedok MRT then bus 401; Eunos MRT then bus 55 or 155 💰 Moderate

SENTOSA CYCLING SERVICES
Bicycle hire on Sentosa Island, with its many cycle tracks, is a fairly relaxing way of getting some exercise, though the routes are popular at weekends.
✚ Off map to south ✉ Sentosa Bicycle Station ☎ 275 0531 🕐 9:30–6:30 🍽 Various food outlets 🚇 ➤ 31 💰 Expensive

FLYING

REPUBLIC OF SINGAPORE FLYING CLUB
If you fancy your hand at flying, try the SFC. Plane rental and training lessons are also available. If, however, it's panoramic aerial views you're after, then sightseeing flights can also be arranged here.
✚ Off map to north ✉ Seletar Air Base, Jalan Kayu, Building 140B, East Camp ☎ 481 0502 🕐 9–6 🚇 Yio Chu Kang MRT then bus 59, 214E 💰 Expensive

GOLF

A day out on the fairway

The Laguna Club has probably the most extensive golf facilities in Singapore, and possibly in Asia. It has two championship 18-hole courses designed by Andy Dye, and an 18-hole putting course, all beautifully landscaped on virgin reclaimed land. The resort's facilities, centred around the clubhouse, make it a good day out even for non-golfing friends and family.

LAGUNA NATIONAL GOLF & COUNTRY CLUB
This golf and country club has two full golf courses: 6,504m, par 73; and 6,210m, par 72. There is also a 550m, par 54, putting course with 18 holes. The club's amenities include a pool, children's playground and playroom, billiards, tennis and a gymnasium.
✚ Off map to east ✉ 11 Laguna Golf Green ☎ 542 6888 🕐 8AM–10PM 🍽 Restaurant, café 🚇 Tanah Merah MRT 💰 Expensive

SELETAR COUNTRY CLUB

This is one of the few country clubs open to non-Singaporeans at weekends. It features a 9-hole, 2,885m, par 35, course set next to Seletar Reservoir to the north of the island.

🚩 Off map to north ✉ 101 Seletar Club Road ☎ 481 4812 ⏰ 7–7 🍴 Restaurant 🚌 59, 103 or 163, then 214 💰 Moderate

ICE-SKATING

ICE WORLD KALLANG

Although it can get crowded at weekends, this centre has reasonable rates and also offers classes for the uninitiated.

🚩 H6 ✉ 5 Stadium Walk, #03-06 ☎ 348 7928 ⏰ Mon–Thu 10–7; Fri–Sat 10–10; Sun 10–6:30 🚌 11, 16 💰 Moderate; around S$12 for two hours with skate hire included

SCUBA DIVING

ASIA AQUATIC

Dive trips and local weekend dives are available here. Other services offered include lessons, equipment sales, rental and repair.

🚩 Off map to west ✉ Block 612, Clementi, West Street 1, #01-302 ☎ 536 8116 ⏰ 9:30–6 🚇 Clementi MRT 💰 Expensive

SENTOSA WATER SPORTS CENTRE

Services offered here include dive trips, day-trips, lessons, and diving equipment sales and rentals. Equipment for other watersports is also available for hire.

🚩 B10 ✉ 1 Maritime Square Suite, #01-06, World Trade Centre ☎ 274 5612 ⏰ 9:30–7 🍴 Various outlets in World Trade Centre 🚇 ► 31 💰 Expensive

WINDSURFING & SAILING

EAST COAST SAILING CENTRE

Basic equipment can be hired here and lessons are available. The beach is fringed with palms and has a bar, shop and café. Barbecues are held on the beach on Sunday and Wednesday evenings.

🚩 Off map to east ✉ East Coast Sailing Lagoon, 1210 East Coast Parkway ☎ 449 5118 ⏰ 10–5 (café closed Mon) 🍴 Café, restaurant, barbecues 🚇 Bedok MRT then bus 31 💰 Moderate

Taking to the waters

With the Riau Islands and the ships in the strait seaward, and the palm-fringed East Coast Park backed by luxury condominiums landward, sailing from the East Coast Sailing Centre offers some spectacular views. The winds are often best in the mid-afternoon, but the tidal currents can be quite strong. The best days end when you come ashore to a barbecue on the beach and the music of a live band.

Watersports are popular in the warm seas around Singapore

ATTRACTIONS FOR CHILDREN

See Top 25 Sights for
SINGAPORE SCIENCE CENTRE ➤ 25
SINGAPORE ZOO ➤ 28

Ring of fire

Although they lie very close to some of the world's most active volcanoes in Indonesia, Singapore and Malaysia did not suffer from this particular hazard. Not, that is, until 1994, when an active volcano miraculously appeared on an island just south of Singapore. There is, however, no cause for alarm. This particular volcano is part of an attraction on Sentosa Island (VolcanoLand), and, despite erupting every half-hour, is perfectly safe.

LAU PA SAT (TELOK AYER MARKET)

This octagonal cast-iron structure, originally a fish market, was built over 100 years ago from pieces shipped out from Scotland. It has been renovated and now houses stalls and kiosks devoted to selling a variety of Asian fare, from Mongolian grilled meats to Hainanese beef noodles. Apart from the food, you'll find stalls selling regional handicrafts such as Balinese carvings and Chinese silks.

dlll/E8 · 18 Raffles Quay 048582 · 11–9 · Foodstalls · Raffles Place MRT

MPH BOOKSTORE

This bookshop is one of Singapore's largest. It is well stocked with books of all types, including many on the region. The music section is on the third floor and there's an extensive children's department on the fourth. Helpfully, it also has its own café.

E6 · 71–7 Stamford Road 178895 · 336 3633 · 10–9:30 · Café · City Hall MRT

TANG DYNASTY VILLAGE

This historical theme park re-creates the 7th-century Chinese city of Chang'An (present-day Xian). Apart from giving visitors a feel for life in the city, the park has a performing Chinese dance troupe and stages traditional festivals. Adding to this hotch potch of Chinese history are life-size replicas of the Xian terracotta warriors from China, and waxworks of notable Chinese figures. Unsurprisingly, the park is often used as a movie lot, so there's always plenty going on.

Off map to west · 2 Yuan Ching Road 618641 · 261 1116 · 10–6:30 · Restaurants · MRT to Lakeside then bus 154 or 240 · Expensive

UNDERWATER WORLD (SENTOSA)

A moving walkway takes you through a glass tunnel, while above and around swim hundreds of species of the region's sea creatures in what is Asia's largest aquarium. This is the closest many will get to a living coral reef, with its strange formations. Look out for the beautiful weedy sea dragon, starfish, poisonous lionfish and sharks.

Off map to south · 80 Siloso Road 098969 · 275 0030 · 9–9 · Restaurant · 31. Bus or monorail from main ferry terminal on Sentosa · Moderate

Tea-time at Singapore Zoo

SINGAPORE
where to...

CHINESE RESTAURANTS

Prices

Approximate prices for an evening meal for one person are as follows:

£ – up to S$20
££ – S$20–S$40
£££ – S$40+

Hokkien variation on a spring roll

Popiah makes a delicious snack. It can be ordered in some restaurants, and most hawker centres have a *popiah* stall. Freshly prepared rice-flour pancakes are filled with a mouthwatering mixture of onion, turnip, beansprouts, minced pork and prawns, all held together with a sweet soy sauce and flavoured with coriander, garlic and chilli. The pancakes usually come ready made, but in some places you can roll your own.

BENG THIN HOON KEE (££)

The Hokkien cuisine here is very popular as the majority of Singapore's Chinese residents are from that region. Duck wrapped in lotus leaves is a particular favourite.

⊞ cII/E7 ⊠ OCBC Building, 65 Chulia Street ☎ 533 7708 ⏲ 11:30–3, 6–10 Ⓜ Raffles Place MRT

DRAGON CITY (££)

Specialities of this well-known Szechuan restaurant include smoked duck, garlic pork and deep-fried shredded beef.

⊞ B3 ⊠ Novotel Orchid Inn, 214 Dunearn Road ☎ 254 5477 ⏲ 11:30–2:30, 6:30–10:30 Ⓜ Newton Road MRT, then bus 171 or 182

FATTY'S EATING HOUSE (££)

A Singapore institution with a wide-ranging Cantonese menu. Everything is well cooked and speedily delivered.

⊞ E5 ⊠ #01-33 Albert Complex, Albert Street ☎ 338 1087 ⏲ 12–2:30, 5:30–10 Ⓜ Bugis MRT

IMPERIAL HERBAL RESTAURANT (£££)

Although not to everyone's taste, this restaurant serves traditional herbal dishes. If you like, a choice of dishes will be suggested to suit your state of health.

⊞ F6 ⊠ Metropole Hotel, 41 Seah Street ☎ 337 0491 ⏲ 11:30–2:30, 6:30–10:30 Ⓜ City Hall MRT

MIN JIANG SICHUAN RESTAURANT (££)

Classic spicy Szechuan food is served here, such as tea-smoked duck and drunken chicken.

⊞ C5 ⊠ Goodwood Park Hotel, 22 Scotts Road ☎ 737 7411 ⏲ 12–2:30, 6:30–10:30 Ⓜ Orchard Road MRT

MOSQUE STREET STEAMBOAT HOUSE AND RESTAURANT (££)

Steamboat, a sort of Chinese fondue, is good value and great fun. Simply choose what you want, cook it in the steamboat stock and eat it, and then finish off with the resulting soup.

⊞ bII/E8 ⊠ 44 Mosque Street ☎ 222 9560 ⏲ 6–6 Ⓜ Tanjong Pagar MRT

SOUP RESTAURANT (££)

The name is misleading as the menu offers a lot more homely Cantonese dishes than just herbal soup. Be sure to try the excellent *samsui* ginger chicken – poached chicken served with a minced ginger dip.

⊞ bII/D8 ⊠ 25 Smith Street ☎ 222 9923 ⏲ 12–2:30, 5:30–9:30 Ⓜ Outram Park MRT

WAK LOK CANTONESE RESTAURANT (££)

Tasty *dim sum* is served here at lunch-times. This, reputedly, is where Hong Kong Chinese come to eat.

⊞ E6 ⊠ Carlton Hotel, 76 Bras Basah Road ☎ 330 3588 ⏲ Mon–Sat 11:30–2:30; Sun 11–2:30, 6:30–10:30 Ⓜ City Hall MRT

INDIAN RESTAURANTS

ANNALAKSHMI (££)

South Indian vegetarian restaurant, part of an Indian arts foundation. Good-value buffet and interesting dips made from mustard and coconut are served with most meals. Try one of their range of drinks.

✚ E7 ✉ #02-10 Excelsior Hotel Shopping Centre, 5 Coleman Street ☎ 339 9993 🕔 Mon–Sat 11:30–3, 6–9:30 🚇 City Hall MRT

BANANA LEAF APOLLO (££)

A banana-leaf restaurant – the leaf takes the place of a plate – with a good range of dishes to accompany the vegetable curries.

✚ E5 ✉ 56 Race Course Road ☎ 293 8682 🕔 10:30–10 🚇 Bugis MRT

KINARA (££)

Northwest Frontier food (north Indian) served in what looks like the inside of a Rajasthani fort makes eating here a memorable experience. The food is good, though helpings can be a little small.

✚ dl/E7 ✉ 57 Boat Quay ☎ 533 0412 🕔 Mon–Fri 12–2:30, 6:30–10:30; Sat–Sun 6:30–10:45 🚇 Raffles Place MRT

KOMALA VILAS (£)

Good, cheap vegetarian food is served here on banana leaves. Basic meals comprise vegetable curries and rice or *dosai* (thin pancakes). A range of snacks is also on offer, or try the sweet, spicy tea – *masala* tea. Upstairs is a small dining-room with air-conditioning.

✚ E5 ✉ 76 Serangoon Road ☎ 293 6980 🕔 7AM–10:30PM 🚇 Bugis MRT

MADRAS NEW WOODLANDS (£)

Similar fare to that available at Komala Vilas. *Thali* is popular here and there is a range of Indian sweetmeats.

✚ E5 ✉ 14 Upper Dickson Road ☎ 297 1594 🕔 7:30AM–11:30PM 🚇 Bugis MRT

MUTHU'S CURRY HOUSE (££)

Vegetable curries are dished out fast and furiously to accompany whatever meat or fish you've ordered. You have to be quick to turn down second helpings! Try the famous fish-head curry.

✚ E5 ✉ 78 Race Course Road ☎ 293 2389 🕔 10–10 🚇 Bugis MRT

NIRVANA (££)

This is the sister restaurant of the famed Moti Mahal on Murray Street, and offers a similar menu of north Indian tandoori dishes.

✚ F4 ✉ 2 Owen Road ☎ 297 0400 🕔 10:30–2:30, 6:30–11 🚇 Lavender Street MRT

RANG MAHAL (£££)

A good range of north Indian dishes and an extensive buffet at both lunch and dinner. Indian dance performances.

✚ D6 ✉ Imperial Hotel, 1 Jalan Rumbia ☎ 737 1666 🕔 12–2:30, 7–11 🚇 Dhoby Ghaut MRT

Saving on the washing-up

Many Indians eat their food with the right hand only; it is considered unclean to eat with the left hand or with utensils. Pieces of chapati are torn using only one hand and used to soak or scoop up elements of the meal. For rice there's another technique: the curries are added to it and the mixture worked up into balls which are then picked up and popped – almost flicked – into the mouth.

SOUTHEAST ASIAN & JAPANESE RESTAURANTS

'Satay! Satay!'

No trip to Singapore would be complete without tasting the famous *satay*, a Malay dish. Sticks of chicken, mutton or beef, and sometimes other foods such as tofu, are barbecued and served with a thick, sweet peanut sauce. Small rice cakes and cucumber usually accompany the *satay*. It is served in some restaurants, and at hawker centres there is nearly always a '*satay* man'. If you develop a taste for it, look in one of the supermarkets for the ready-made *satay* sauce and try it at home with a barbecue.

AZIZAS (££)

One of Singapore's best Malay restaurants. Try beef *rendang* (beef cooked in coconut milk), or a fish dish.

✚ E5 ✉ #02-15 Albert Court, 180 Albert Street ☎ 235 1130 🕐 Mon–Sat 11:30–2:30 🚇 Bugis MRT

HAE BOK'S KOREAN RESTAURANT (££)

Serves a wide range of reliably good Korean dishes with either Korean or ginseng tea.

✚ C7 ✉ 405 Havelock Road #02-20 ☎ 223 9004 🕐 11:30–3, 5:30–10 🚇 Tiong Bahru MRT

HOUSE OF SUNDANESE FOOD (££)

Spicy food from west Java – the fish dishes are particularly good. The original restaurant is at 218 East Coast Road ☎ 345 5020, and another newer outlet is in the Suntec City Mall basement ☎ 334 8660.

✚ dI/E7 ✉ 55 Boat Quay ☎ 534 3775 🕐 Mon–Fri 11–2; Sat 12–2:30, 6–10 🚇 Raffles Place MRT

INAGIKU (£££)

Has four sections serving very good-quality *tempura*, *teppanyaki*, *sushi* and an à la carte menu, the latter being the cheapest option.

✚ F6 ✉ 3rd floor, Westin Plaza Hotel, 2 Stamford Road ☎ 338 8585 🕐 Mon–Sat 12–2:30, 6:30–10:30 🚇 City Hall MRT

NONYA AND BABA (££)

Dishes such as *otak-otak* (fish cakes in banana leaves) and *itek tim* (duck soup) are typical examples of *nonya* food (► 33). The rice- and coconut-based desserts are worth trying, but the agar jellies are an acquired taste!

✚ D6 ✉ 262 River Valley Road ☎ 734 1382 🕐 11–3, 6–10 🚇 Dhoby Ghaut MRT 🚌 32, 54, 195

SUNTORY (££)

This long-established Japanese restaurant is expensive but good. Serves excellent *sushi*, *tempura* and *shabu-shabu*.

✚ C5 ✉ #06-01 Delfi Orchard, 402 Orchard Road ☎ 732 5111 🕐 12–3, 6:30–11 🚇 Orchard Road MRT

TAMBUAH MAS (££)

This excellent restaurant serves very good Indonesian food. Don't miss the *ikan bilis* (whitebait and peanuts) and *soto ayam* (thick chicken soup) – almost Java's national dish. A second branch is at the Shaw Centre (5th floor).

✚ B5 ✉ #04-10 Tanglin Shopping Centre, 19 Tanglin Road ☎ 733 2220 🕐 10–10 🚇 Orchard MRT

THANYING (££)

This Thai restaurant is always packed out – try the green curries and stuffed chicken wings.

✚ bIV/D9 ✉ Amara Hotel, 165 Tanjong Pagar Road ☎ 222 4688/227 7856 🕐 Mon–Sat 11:30–3, 6:30–11 🚇 Tanjong Pagar MRT

HAWKER CENTRES

CHINA SQUARE (£)

A sprawling new three-storey food complex that has Western food outlets and traditional hawker fare all under one roof.

cII/E8 ✉ Telok Ayer Street 🕐 7AM–10PM 🚇 Raffles Place MRT

CHINATOWN COMPLEX FOOD CENTRE (£)

This large food centre, in the midst of Chinatown, is always buzzing. Most types of local Chinese food are available here, as is a wide range of desserts – try the ice *kacang*.

bII/D8 ✉ Chinatown Complex, Smith Street 🕐 Early till late 🚇 Outram Park MRT

EAST COAST LAGOON FOOD CENTRE (£)

The good food and sea breezes make this a popular dining spot. The *satay* is very good, as is the *laksa* and any number of tantalising seafood dishes such as chilli or black pepper crab, stuffed squid and cuttlefish.

✚ Off map to east ✉ East Coast Parkway 🕐 Late morning till late 🚇 Bugis MRT, then bus 401 (Sat/Sun/holidays only)

MAXWELL ROAD (£)

This hawker centre is nicely old-fashioned – not many bright lights or mod cons. The food is good, especially some of the basics like chicken rice and *murtabak*.

bIII/E8 ✉ Corner of Maxwell Road and South Bridge Road 🕐 Early till late 🚇 Tanjong Pagar MRT

NEWTON CIRCUS (£)

Probably the most expensive of the hawker centres, and popular with coach-borne tourists. More than 100 stalls offer every type of local food. Lobster is good, and try the 'carrot cake'!

D5 ✉ Clemenceau Avenue 🕐 24 hours 🚇 Newton MRT

TAMAN SERASI (£)

This small hawker centre, near the Botanic Gardens, serves excellent fruit juices and *roti john*, a Malay dish like a savoury mince sandwich.

A5 ✉ Cluny Road 🕐 6AM–8PM 🚇 Orchard MRT

SCOTTS (£)

This air-conditioned food court in a shopping-centre basement is handy for a shopping lunch. A variety of stalls include Korean, Thai and vegetarian options.

C5 ✉ Picnic Food Court, Scotts, Scotts Road 🕐 Sun–Thu 10:30–10; Fri, Sat and eve of public hols 10:30–10:30 🚇 Orchard MRT

ZHUJIAO FOOD CENTRE (£)

This food centre, in the middle of a bustling market, makes a good place to watch the world go by. Try getting up early and having an Indian breakfast here of *roti prata* and sweet milky coffee.

E5 ✉ Zhujiao Food Market (KK Market), Serangoon Road 🕐 Early till late 🚇 Bugis MRT

Popular orders – at a glance

Char kway teow Flat noodles with prawns, pork and beansprouts.

Beef kway teow Flat noodles with beef.

Chicken rice As it sounds!

Laksa Rice noodles and prawns in coconut milk.

Mee goreng Fried spicy noodles.

Nasi biryani Rice and spiced chicken or mutton.

Murtabak Pancake with minced beef or mutton.

Chilli crab Crab, chilli and tomato sauce, garlic; served in the shell.

Ice kacang Red beans, jelly, sweetcorn, ice and evaporated milk.

Bandung Rose syrup and milk – it's the lurid pink drink!

ITALIAN RESTAURANTS

A taste of Italy

It seems that Italian food really does travel well: a few years ago there were very few Italian restaurants in Singapore; now there are scores. New ones are springing up all the time and, apart from the individual restaurants, chains such as Pizza Hut and Milano's also do extremely well. So if you're craving something other than rice or noodles, you'll have no difficulty finding fresh pasta and pizzas almost anywhere in Singapore.

AL FORNO TRATTORIA (££)

A popular restaurant, though a little way out of the centre, so book. Antipasto and pizzas are particularly good.
✚ D4 ✉ #01-05 Goldhill Plaza, Thompson Road ☎ 256 2848 ⏱ Noon–2, 6:30–10:30. Closed Sun 🚇 Novena MRT

IL PICCOLO (££)

Though small in size, this diner-style, or neighbourhood, restaurant is big in flavour. It offers a good selection of pastas, pizzas and desserts
✚ Off map to north-west ✉ 557 Bukit Timah Road, #01-06 Crown Centre ☎ 468 5837 ⏱ Noon–2:30, 6:30–10. Closed Mon 🚇 MRT to Newton then bus 66, 67, 74, 151, 154, 156, 157, 170, 171, 174

LA FORKETTA (££)

A little off the beaten track, on the second floor of a small shopping centre, but it's worth finding as the food, especially the pizzas, is very good.
✚ Off map to west ✉ 3 South Buona Vista Road, #02-03 ☎ 778 8873 ⏱ 12–2:30, 6–10. Closed Mon 🚌 10, 30, 43

PASTA BRAVA (££)

Lovely restaurant in a converted shop house on the edge of Chinatown. Some dishes can be expensive, but the food is very good. Especially popular at lunch-times.
✚ bIII/D8 ✉ 11 Craig Road ☎ 227 7550 ⏱ 11:30–2:30, 6:30–10:30 🚇 Tanjong Pagar MRT

PETE'S PLACE (£££)

Pete's Place has been established for a number of years and is popular with visitors and locals. The pasta dishes are tasty, and an excellent salad bar makes it a good place for vegetarians.
✚ C5 ✉ Basement, Hyatt Regency Singapore, 10–12 Scotts Road ☎ 738 1234 ⏱ 11:30–2:30, 6–11 🚇 Orchard MRT

PREGO (££)

Popular both at lunch-time and in the evenings for its excellent range of dishes and central location. Also has a take-away deli counter.
✚ F7 ✉ Westin Stamford Hotel, 2 Stamford Road ☎ 431 5156 ⏱ Noon–2:30, 6:30–10:30 🚇 City Hall MRT

PRONTO (££)

An open-air restaurant beside the Oriental hotel's fifth-floor pool. The *antipasti misto* is good, but leave room for the delicious tiramisu.
✚ F7 ✉ The Oriental Singapore, 5 Raffles Avenue ☎ 331 0551 ⏱ 11–2:30, 6–10:30 🚇 City Hall MRT

ROCKY'S (££)

It's possible you may just feel like a take-away pizza, and if so Rocky's is the best in town. Allow an hour for delivery. There are two branches.
✚ L5 ✉ 419 East Coast Road ☎ 440 9112 ⏱ 11–10:30 (last order 10) 🚇 Eunos MRT. ✚ Off map to west ✉ 61 Sunset Way, Clementi Park Shopping Centre ☎ 344 6868 ⏱ As above 🚇 Clementi MRT

OTHER WESTERN RESTAURANTS

ALKAFF MANSION (£££)

An expensive restaurant, but worth the price for the setting alone. A 1920s colonial house sitting atop a hill in the west of the city has been turned into a charming restaurant. International cuisine is available, plus *rijstaffel* – Indonesian-Dutch buffet.

🏠 A8 ✉ 10 Telok Blangah Green ☎ 278 6979 ◷ Noon–2:30 (lunch), 3–5:30 (high tea), 7–10:30 (dinner) 🚌 124, 143, 166

BRAZIL CHURRASCARIA (££)

Possibly Singapore's only Brazilian eating place. For a set price you can choose from an extensive and interesting salad bar and then take as many as you like of the succulent spit-roasted cuts of meat brought to your table in rapid succession. Not for vegetarians!

🏠 Off map to west ✉ 14/16 Sixth Avenue, just off Bukit Timah Road ☎ 463 1923 ◷ 11:45–2:30, 6:30–10:30 🚇 Newton MRT then bus 156, 170, 174

CHA CHA CHA (££)

A bright and cheerful Mexican restaurant in Holland Village. The cheese and mushroom *burritos* are particularly tasty and good.

🏠 Off map to west ✉ 32 Lorong Mambong, Holland Village ☎ 462 1650 ◷ Noon–11 🚌 61, 106

HARD ROCK CAFÉ (££)

Steaks and hamburgers are the most popular items on the menu at this large music bar, part of the international chain.

🏠 C5 ✉ #02-01 HPL House, 50 Cuscaden Road ☎ 235 6256 ◷ 11–10:30 (for food) 🚇 Orchard MRT

J P BASTIANI (££)

Mediterranean food – mainly Italian, Greek and Spanish – is served in plush surroundings in a restored godown on Clarke Quay. Downstairs there is a cool, comfy bar for aperitifs and coffee.

🏠 E7 ✉ A01-12 Clarke Quay ☎ 433 0156 ◷ 11:30–2:30, 6–11 🚇 City Hall MRT 🚌 32, 54, 195

LATOUR (£££)

This French restaurant, in one of Singapore's leading and most expensive hotels, is only for special occasions. Meals are costly, but quality, service and the ambience are excellent.

🏠 B5 ✉ Ground Floor, Shangri-La Hotel, 22 Orange Grove Road ☎ 730 2471 ◷ Noon–2:30, 6:30–10:30 🚇 Orchard MRT

PAULANER BRÄUHAUS (££)

German theme restaurant-cum-brewery serving generous platters of *wurst kartoffein* and sauerkraut. There are two branches.

🏠 F7 ✉ #01-01 Millennia Walk, 9 Raffles Boulevard ☎ 337 7123 ◷ 11:30–2:30, 6–10 (drinks only after 10) 🚇 City Hall MRT 🏠 C5 ✉ 501 Orchard Road ☎ 737 8884 ◷ As above 🚇 Orchard MRT

Dinner is served

For a romantic evening, far from the hustle and bustle of Orchard Road or a hawker centre, you can't beat the breezy hilltop terrace of the Alkaff Mansion on Telok Blangah Green. It's a lovely spot for an aperitif, or a coffee after your meal. The restored rooms, hung with huge mirrors upstairs and down, make for wonderful, old-fashioned dining-rooms. Don't also miss the charming bathrooms! If you're keen to take full advantage of the terrace during daylight hours, the restaurant also serves a delicious high tea.

VEGETARIAN RESTAURANTS & DO-IT-YOURSELF OPTIONS

What's for afters?

While Singapore may not be known for its apple pies and cream tortes, it does have something just as tempting – tropical fruits. Here's a rundown of some of the favourites:

Durian Not for the fainthearted! This huge spiky fruit, when opened, reveals a creamy-yellow, soft, slimy interior, which smells quite obnoxious. However, if you can overcome that the taste is not unpleasant.

Guava Looking like huge pears, guavas usually have a pink granular flesh that is used to make a thick, sweet drink.

Rambutan This small, red, hairy fruit is most delicious. The fruit is sold in bunches and the firm, white flesh is sweet and rather like that of a lychee.

Papaya This large marrow-shaped fruit is traditionally served for breakfast with lime juice and is rich in vitamin A.

VEGETARIAN DRAGON PARK (££)

A great variety of dishes is on offer here. Don't be put off by the mock meat as it's all vegetarian fare.

⊞ bII/E8 ⊠ 18 Mosque Street, #01-02 Dragon Inn Chinatown ☎ 224 2533 ⏰ 11:30–2:30, 6–10 🚇 Outram Park MRT

FUT SAI KAI VEGETARIAN RESTAURANT (££)

Few Chinese are vegetarians, but this unusual restaurant serves Buddhist cuisine. Obviously, lots of vegetables are on the menu, as are tofu and soyabean dishes, often shaped to resemble cuts of meat or fish.

⊞ F5 ⊠ 143 Kitchener Road ☎ 298 0336 ⏰ 10–9 🚇 Bugis MRT

LINGZHI VEGETARIAN RESTAURANT (£)

This vegetarian restaurant has both a busy take-away counter and an eat-in area with a Chinese courtyard-like look. Popular dishes such as braised spinach, barbecued mushrooms and braised beancurd skin roll disappear quickly at this well-patronised restaurant.

⊞ C5 ⊠ #B1-17/18 Orchard Towers, 400 Orchard Road ☎ 734 3788 ⏰ 11:30–3, 6–10 🚇 Orchard MRT

OLIO DOME (££)

This Australian restaurant serves an exciting range of salads, foccacia bread sandwiches and other snacks – lots of possibilities for vegetarians.

⊞ C5 ⊠ Level 3, Wheelock Place, 501 Orchard Road ☎ 737 6958 ⏰ 10:30–10:30 🚇 Orchard MRT

ORIGINAL SIN (££)

Completely vegetarian menu at this Mediterranean-style restaurant. The imaginative use of ingredients gives run-of-the-mill dishes a real twist.

⊞ Off map to west ⊠ Block 43, Jalan Merah Saga, #01-62 Chip Bee Gardens, Holland Village ☎ 475 5605 ⏰ Tue–Sun 11:30–2:30, 6–10:30; Mon 6–10:30 🚌 5, 7, 61, 106

SRI VIJAYA (£)

Modest vegetarian banana-leaf establishment offering great value for money. Generous helpings of rice and vegetable accompaniments.

⊞ E6 ⊠ 229 Selegie Road ☎ 336 1748 ⏰ 7AM–10PM 🚇 Bugis MRT

DO-IT-YOURSELF

If you want provisions for a picnic, these supermarkets should have all you need:

COLD STORAGE CENTREPOINT

⊞ D6 ⊠ #B1-14 Centrepoint, 176 Orchard Road ☎ 737 4222 ⏰ 9AM–10PM 🚇 Somerset MRT

JASON'S SUPERMARKET

⊞ C5 ⊠ 1 Claymore Drive, #01-01 Orchard Towers ☎ 235 4355 ⏰ Mon–Sat 8AM–9PM; Sun 9–9 🚇 Orchard MRT

TEA & COFFEE STOPS

AH TENG'S BAKERY (£)

This small café, next to the Empire Café, is just behind Raffles Hotel. Breads, cakes and ice-creams are on offer. Look out for the giant wholemeal muffins – a meal in themselves.

✚ F6 ✉ 1 Beach Road, Raffles Hotel Arcade ☎ 331 1711 ⏰ 8AM–11PM 🚇 City Hall MRT

COFFEE CLUB, HOLLAND VILLAGE (£)

The Coffee Club specialises in serving a vast range of interesting coffees, some with cream and a choice of different spirits.

✚ Off map to west ✉ 27 Lorong Mambong, Holland Village ☎ 466 0296 ⏰ 10AM–11PM 🚌 5, 7, 61, 106

COMPASS ROSE RESTAURANT (££)

High tea, in more senses than one, is served here every day: its location on the 72nd floor makes it one of the world's highest restaurants. Apart from the wonderful spread on offer, enjoy the view.

✚ F7 ✉ Westin Stamford Hotel, 2 Stamford Road ☎ 338 8585 ⏰ Noon–5:30 🚇 City Hall MRT

DELIFRANCE (££)

One of an ever-growing chain of French-style cafés, this establishment, like the rest, serves a variety of filled baguettes and other savouries and sweets.

✚ E7 ✉ #01-03, 11 Stamford Road ☎ 334 1645 ⏰ 7:30AM–10PM 🚇 City Hall MRT

GOODWOOD PARK HOTEL (££)

English tea is served in a light and airy dining-room overlooking the hotel's swimming pool. A pianist is on hand to lend a musical note to the afternoon's indulgences.

✚ C5 ✉ 22 Scotts Road ☎ 737 7411 ⏰ 2:30–6 🚇 Orchard MRT

HILTON HOTEL (££)

The Hilton obviously has a number of first-rate pastry chefs; the cake selection on offer at teatime is a delight. Don't miss the special cheesecakes.

✚ C5 ✉ 581 Orchard Road ☎ 737 2233 ⏰ 3–6 🚇 Orchard MRT

RAFFLES HOTEL (££)

A sumptous tea is served in the Tiffin Room and the Bar and Billiard restaurant. It is best to arrive early as this is a popular spot for taking afternoon tea, especially at weekends.

✚ F6 ✉ 1 Beach Road ☎ 337 1886 ⏰ 3:30–5 🚇 City Hall MRT

SPINELLI COFFEE COMPANY (££)

A San Francisco-based outfit that is riding on the crest of Singapore's current coffee craze. It has an open-air location and is ideal for people-watching.

✚ D6 ✉ #01-10, The Heeren, 260 Orchard Road ☎ 738 0233 ⏰ 8AM–10PM 🚇 Somerset MRT

Coffee-shops

Singapore's traditional coffee-shops are nothing like the modern places that sell a sophisticated selection of Javanese coffee and wholemeal brownies. They are no-nonsense, cheap and cheerful eating establishments, where you can get the favourite local rice and noodle dishes. You do also get coffee, but it tends to be of just one type – thick and sweet, made with condensed milk. Mindful of waste, take-away coffees are sometimes served in the empty condensed-milk cans, and you will occasionally see people carrying these, though the more usual coffee container today is a plastic bag, which you can sometimes see tied to knobs or railings while the contents cool down!

ORCHARD ROAD WEST

Changing times

'Beyond the bazaar, ... Orchard Road becomes a straight, well-shaded drive, leading to the European residences in the Tanglin district. On the left, almost hidden by the trees is a very large Chinese Burial Ground formerly used by the Teo Chews, ie Chinese hailing from Swatow. The visitor may perhaps overtake a funeral on its way to one of these Chinese burying grounds in the suburbs, with the customary accompaniments of gongs to startle, and the scattering of gold and silver paper to appease the spirit of the deceased. Orchard Road ends at the entrance to the Military Barracks in Tanglin Road.'
– The Revd G M Reith, *Handbook to Singapore*, 1907, OUP.

TANGLIN MALL
Opened in early 1995, this shopping centre aims to provide something a little different from the proliferation of designer labels on offer elsewhere in Orchard Road. There is a range of shops, including some interesting children's stores, and, in the mall, a handicrafts market is held every third Saturday each month.
✚ B5 ✉ 163 Tanglin Road
☎ 736 4922 ⏰ 10–10
Ⓜ Orchard MRT

TANGLIN SHOPPING CENTRE
This is one of the area's oldest shopping centres. It is well known for its Asian antiques and curios (though, as with most places in Singapore, prices are high). It is also good for carpets and rugs, and for tailoring.
✚ B5 ✉ 19 Tanglin Road
☎ 737 0849 ⏰ 10–6
Ⓜ Orchard MRT

ORCHARD TOWERS
Many small specialist traders fill this centre, known particularly for its jewellery and silk stores. There are also a number of restaurants on the upper floors.
✚ C5 ✉ 400 Orchard Road
☎ 734 5922 ⏰ 9:30AM–10PM
Ⓜ Orchard MRT

WHEELOCK PLACE
This striking and ideally located centre is very popular. A vast Borders bookshop takes up much of the ground floor, and Marks & Spencer occupies the basement. There's even an organic food store.
✚ C5 ✉ 501 Orchard Road
⏰ Sun–Thu 10:30–8:30; Fri–Sat 10:30–9:30
Ⓜ Orchard MRT

SHAW CENTRE
This office-cum-small-shops centre is linked to Shaw House (see below) and has a number of interesting outlets, including a reasonably priced shoe shop (Fairlady), a small clothes shop (Solo) and a number of gift shops. Usefully, there is even a hardware store (Handyman Centre).
✚ C5 ✉ 1 Scotts Road
☎ 737 9080 ⏰ 10–10
Ⓜ Orchard MRT

SHAW HOUSE
This is a very useful shopping centre with a well-stocked department store, basement supermarket, cafés and a five-screen cinema on the top floor.
✚ C5 ✉ 350 Orchard Road
☎ 737 9080 ⏰ 10–10
Ⓜ Orchard MRT

PACIFIC PLAZA
Pacific Plaza is another new and 'in' place for Singapore's youth. Venom is a nightclub people will seemingly queue for hours to get into, and Tower Records, on the fourth floor, provides what is probably Singapore's largest selection of popular music.
✚ C5 ✉ 9 Scotts Road
☎ 733 5655 ⏰ 10–10
Ⓜ Orchard MRT

ORCHARD ROAD EAST

FAR EAST PLAZA
Boasting more than 800 outlets, this is one of Singapore's most popular centres, offering almost everything, from clothes to haircuts and from compact discs to shoe repairs.
✚ C5 ✉ 14 Scotts Road ☎ 734 2325 ⏰ 10–9 Ⓜ Orchard MRT

SCOTTS
This relatively small shopping centre is very good for fashion items. With the PicnicFood Court in the basement and a SISTIC counter on the second floor for theatre tickets, it's a handy emporium.
✚ C5 ✉ 6 Scotts Road ☎ 734 7560 ⏰ 10–9 (food court 10–10) Ⓜ Orchard MRT

TANGS
Situated half-way along Orchard Road, this is one of Singapore's most popular department stores and is a useful meeting point. A ground-floor department sells 'ethnic' clothes, and a number of 'curio corners' are useful for gift shopping.
✚ C5 ✉ 320 Orchard Road ☎ 737 5500 ⏰ Mon–Fri 11–9; Sat 11–9:30; Sun 12:30–8 Ⓜ Orchard MRT

LUCKY PLAZA
Another huge shopping complex, full of small stores selling all manner of goods. The salespeople may be aggressive – so bargain!
✚ C5 ✉ 304 Orchard Road ☎ 235 3294 ⏰ 9–9 Ⓜ Orchard MRT

NGEE ANN CITY
(➤ 32)

THE HEEREN
One of the latest centres on Orchard Road for the hip and trendy. Be seen browsing the three floors of HMV or sipping coffee at Spinelli's outdoor café (➤ 69).
✚ D6 ✉ 260 Orchard Road ☎ 733 4725 ⏰ 10AM–11PM Ⓜ Somerset MRT

SPECIALISTS' SHOPPING CENTRE
One of Singapore's older shopping centres, offering a range of boutiques and small stores. Primarily known for the John Little department store.
✚ D6 ✉ 277 Orchard Road ☎ 737 8222 ⏰ 10:30–8:30 Ⓜ Somerset MRT

CENTREPOINT
Centrepoint is one of Singapore's most user-friendly centres. There's a good department store, and a host of interesting shops selling everything from books to clothes and electrical goods, plus a supermarket, restaurants and cafés.
✚ D6 ✉ 176 Orchard Road ☎ 235 6629 ⏰ 10:30–9 Ⓜ Somerset MRT

CUPPAGE TERRACE
As a relief from large, glitzy shopping centres, Cuppage Terrace offers a small selection of arts and crafts shops. Near by are lots of reasonably priced eateries.
✚ D6 ✉ 55 Cuppage Road ⏰ 10–7 Ⓜ Somerset MRT

Top to toe
Need a haircut? Try Toni & Guy (✉ #02-03/04 Pacific Plaza, 9 Scotts Road ☎ 732 4486) or Passion (✉ #02-09/10 The Promenade, 300 Orchard Road ☎ 733 5638). And what about some new shoes? Try Le Saunda (✉ #01-19/20 Scotts Shopping Centre, 6 Scotts Road ☎ 733 6086) or On Pedder (✉ #02-12F/P/Q Ngee Ann City, 319 Orchard Road ☎ 835 1307).

CHINATOWN & THE SINGAPORE RIVER

BOAT QUAY

There are not too many shops on this stretch of the river, rather more restaurants. One good place for browsing, prior to dining, is Tower Books at 82 Boat Quay, which stocks some European-language books.

✚ c/d1/E7 ✉ Boat Quay
Ⓜ Raffles Place MRT

CHINATOWN POINT

One of Chinatown's largest shopping centres, containing a great variety of shops and eateries, and specialising in local handicraft and gift shops.

✚ b11/D8 ✉ 133 New Bridge Road ☎ 534 0112 Ⓒ 10–10
Ⓜ Outram Park MRT

CLARKE QUAY & RIVERSIDE POINT
(► 35)

FUNAN CENTRE

This shopping complex, recently 'retrofitted', specialises in computers (more than 70 shops) and photographic equipment shops, though, of course, as with most of Singapore's shopping centres, much else is on offer.

✚ E7 ✉ 109 North Bridge Road ☎ 336 8327
Ⓒ 11–7/8 Ⓜ City Hall MRT

PEOPLE'S PARK COMPLEX

All manner of goods can be bought in this bustling centre in the heart of Chinatown. It is one of the oldest of Singapore's shopping centres and has a very local character. There

are lots of food and drink stalls if you need a break from bargain-hunting.

✚ b11/D8 ✉ 1 Park Road
☎ 535 9533 Ⓒ 10–9:30
Ⓜ Outram Park MRT

PIDEMCO CENTRE

The Pidemco Centre houses Singapore's Jewellery Mart, and is a good starting point to see the range and cost of jewellery available here.

✚ c1/E7 ✉ South Bridge Road
☎ 539 7721 Ⓒ 10:30–6.
Closed Sun Ⓜ City Hall MRT

TEMPLE/PAGODA/ TRENGGANU STREETS

In the streets between South Bridge Road and New Bridge Road, in the heart of Chinatown, shops and stalls sell a tantalising range of Chinese goods: herbal remedies, exotic fruit, gold jewellery and porcelain. The rich smell of a great Chinese favourite, barbecued pork, pervades the streets.

✚ b11/E8 ✉ Temple Street off South Bridge Road Ⓜ Outram Park MRT

YUE HWA CHINESE PRODUCTS EMPORIUM

This well laid-out department store in the heart of Chinatown has a great array of good-quality goods, from traditional and modern clothes to handicrafts and food and household items.

✚ b11/D8 ✉ 70 Eu Tong Sen Street ☎ 538 9233 Ⓒ 11–10
Ⓜ Outram Park MRT

ARAB STREET & LITTLE INDIA

ALBERT STREET
Start off at the Albert Complex and work your way up to Albert Court (Selegie Road end), where two rows of shop houses have been renovated and now contain gift shops and eateries. Side-street detours to stalls are worth taking.

✚ E5 🚇 Bugis MRT

ARAB STREET
A great variety of good-quality handicrafts can be bought in this area. In particular, look out for the basketware, textiles, jewellery and perfume – all of which come in a myriad of forms. This is the best area in Singapore for buying fabric, with numerous shops offering silks, cottons and batiks in profusion.

✚ F6 ✉ Area bounded by Jalan Sultan, Beach Road, Ophir Road and Victoria Street
🚇 Bugis MRT

DUNLOP STREET
Bursting with colourful provisions, textiles and fancy-goods shops, Dunlop Street encapsulates the atmosphere of Little India. Packets of spices and Indian soaps make interesting, lightweight gifts.

✚ E5 🚇 Bugis MRT

LITTLE INDIA ARCADE
Another redevelopment project where a stretch of old shop houses has been gentrified into a shopping complex. This one, being at the gateway to Little India, has a totally Indian feel and is worth visiting for its restaurants and for its shops, these selling textiles, jewellery, ayurvedic medicines, garlands and spices.

✚ E5 ✉ 48 Serangoon Road
☎ 295 5998 🕐 9–9 (restaurants 9AM–11PM)
🚇 Bugis MRT

SERANGOON PLAZA
This busy emporium is always packed with Indians, both local and visitors, stocking up on everything from food to electrical items and cosmetics. It's particularly good for cheap everyday clothes and household goods.

✚ F5 ✉ 320 Serangoon Road
☎ 296 4196 🕐 10–10
🚇 Bugis MRT

SIM LIM SQUARE
(► 77)

ZHUJIAO MARKET (KK MARKET)
The ground floor of this busy market is just the place for fruit and flowers. On the second floor, above the food sellers, you'll find a range of clothes, textiles and luggage. The quality isn't the finest but it's a good place for bargains and unusual items – such as Chinese babywear.

✚ E5 ✉ Buffalo Road
🕐 10–7 🚇 Bugis MRT

Perfumers' corner

At the North Bridge Road end of Arab Street it is possible to buy scents made from a heady mixture of essences: attar of rose, sandalwood, jasmine, honeysuckle and other gorgeously scented ingredients. The perfumes come in beautiful glass bottles and, depending upon your blend, can be quite expensive. But it may be worth treating yourself as the scents are very strong and a little goes a long way.

HANDICRAFTS & ANTIQUES

Hour-old antiques

Singapore has a plethora of antique and reproduction shops, but buyers should beware and purchase only from reputable dealers. Furniture and artefacts over 100 years old are considered antiques. A reputable dealer will give a certificate of antiquity or a detailed description along with a receipt. This type of proof may be required to ensure duty-free importation. If you are travelling throughout Southeast Asia, you'll find prices are usually lower in the country of origin than in Singapore, but shipping charges and importation duties can add up. Prices in Singapore vary widely, and bargaining is essential.

ANTIQUES OF THE ORIENT

You could spend hours browsing through this shop's fine selection of old lithographs, prints, maps and antique books.

B5 ✉ #02-40 Tanglin Shopping Centre, 19 Tanglin Road ☎ 734 9351 🕐 Mon–Sat 10–6; Sun 10:30–4:30 🚇 Orchard MRT

BABAZAR

Babazar offers inviting and uncluttered displays, ranging from items as small as Christmas tree decorations right up to massive pieces of furniture. The collection includes artefacts from all over Asia.

D6 ✉ 31A Cuppage Terrace ☎ 235 7866 🕐 10–6. Closed Sun 🚇 Somerset MRT

LAVANYA

Textiles, small carvings, traditional furniture and jewellery are among the samplings on offer in this centrally located shop.

E7 ✉ #02-11 Excelsior Hotel and Shopping Centre, 5 Coleman Street ☎ 339 8572 🕐 10–9. Closed Sun 🚇 City Hall MRT

LIM'S ARTS & CRAFTS

A wide selection of handicrafts, including linens, jewellery, pottery and silk pyjamas, line the shelves of this shop. Popular with expats.

Off map to west ✉ #02-01 Holland Road Shopping Centre, 211 Holland Avenue ☎ 467 1300 🕐 Mon–Sat 9:30–8:30; Sun, public hols 10:30–6:30 🚌 5, 7, 61, 106

MATA-HARI

Basketry, lacquerware and silver jewellery are among the shop's arts and crafts, originating from Burma, Thailand, Cambodia, Vietnam and Indonesia.

B5 ✉ #02-26 Tanglin Shopping Centre, 19 Tanglin Road ☎ 737 6068 🕐 10:30–6:30. Closed Sun 🚇 Orchard MRT

MUSEUM SHOP

A lovely selection of handicrafts from South and Southeast Asia is displayed well here: woven baskets from Lombok, silver jewellery, shawls and sarongs are examples.

E6 ✉ 53 Armenian Street ☎ 332 3629 🕐 9:30–6:30. Closed Mon 🚇 City Hall MRT

POLAR ARTS OF ASIA

Treasures from throughout Asia are jam-packed into this shop. Plates and pots from Nepal, Burma and the Thai hill tribes, spears from Papua New Guinea and gourd penis sheaths are just a few of the eye-catching items.

C5 ✉ #02-16 Far East Shopping Centre, Orchard Road ☎ 734 2311 🕐 11–6. Closed Sun 🚇 Orchard MRT

SINGAPORE HANDICRAFT CENTRE

The Handicraft Centre, in Chinatown's heart, includes five floors of shops where all manner of curios may be found, including antique snuff bottles, carpets and calligraphic works.

bII/D8 ✉ Chinatown Point, 133 New Bridge Road 🕐 10–10 🚇 Outram Park MRT

EASTERN TRADING GOODS

ALJUNIED BROTHERS HOUSE OF BATIK

One of many good batik shops on Arab Street, Aljunied carries not only batik fabric but also ready-made dresses, shirts, tablecloths, stuffed toys and the like in batik.

⊞ F6 ✉ 91 Arab Street
☎ 293 2751 🕒 9:30–6.
Closed Sun 🚇 Bugis MRT

BATIK CORNER

Briefcases, camera cases and purses are just some of the leather items on offer here. There's a good selection of batik, too.

⊞ F6 ✉ #01-19 Golden Landmark Hotel, 390 Victoria Street ☎ 291 4467
🕒 10–8:30 🚇 Bugis MRT

EAST INDIA TRADING COMPANY

For cotton tops and trousers, both men's and women's, the East India Trading Company is the place to visit. Prices are not cheap but both the quality and the range are quite good.

⊞ E6 ✉ 11 Stamford Road
☎ 336 0332 🕒 11:30–9
🚇 City Hall MRT

EASTERN CARPETS

The walls and floors of this shop are covered with Persian and Pakistani carpets, offering shoppers a wide selection to choose from. Classes in carpet appreciation are also available.

⊞ F6 ✉ #03-26/7 Raffles City Shopping Centre, 252 North Bridge Road ☎ 338 8135
🕒 10:30–9:30 🚇 City Hall MRT

POPPY FABRIC

All the colours of the rainbow are reflected in the Thai and Chinese silks sold in this store and in others along Arab Street.

⊞ F5 ✉ 111 Arab Street
☎ 293 3143 🕒 10–6. Closed Sun 🚇 Bugis MRT

RAHMATH TRADING CORPORATION

In Arab bazaar fashion, this shop is bursting with rattan and wicker items of every sort: mats, baskets, fans, magazine racks, chests and even babycarriers.

⊞ F5 ✉ 25 Arab Street
☎ 298 4553 🕒 9–6. Closed Sun 🚇 Bugis MRT

SELECT BOOK SHOP

For books on the region this is the best shop. It stocks a wide range of guides, beautiful coffee-table books on subjects as diverse as natural history, cuisine and architecture, and a range of specialist academic texts and papers on regional themes.

⊞ B5 ✉ #03-15/17 Tanglin Shopping Centre, 19 Tanglin Road ☎ 732 1515
🕒 9:30–6:30. Closed Sun
🚇 Orchard MRT

THANDAPANI

Locals and expats alike come to these spice shops in Little India.

⊞ E5 ✉ 124 Dunlop Street
☎ 292 3163 🕒 9–9
🚇 Bugis MRT

Carpet auctions

Taking in a carpet auction can be a fun way to spend a Sunday. Several carpet companies hold auctions on Sundays, usually at the Hyatt, the Hilton or the Holiday Inn. Carpets are spread out for easy viewing from about 10AM until just after noon. Estimated market prices are posted and a Continental-type buffet breakfast is often offered free to participants. Auctions usually start about 1PM. Depending on the number of viewers and the thickness of their wallets, bidding proceeds at a fast pace. Expect to get 50–70 per cent off the estimated price, or at least start the bidding there.

WATCHES & JEWELLERY

Jade

The written Chinese character for jade signifies beauty, nobility and purity, and the stone is much valued by the Chinese. The value of jade lies in its colour, texture and translucent appearance. The most common types are nephrite and jadeite, both of which are very hard and cold to the touch. Nephrite is paler than the more vivid jadeite. And green is not the only colour for the stone: it comes in many hues, ranging from several shades of green to pure white and lavender.

APOLLO GOLDSMITHS PTE LTD

This is just one of many shops that sell gold jewellery along Buffalo Road and Serangoon Road. Gold is sold by the gram, so any difference in cost is due to the design and work.
✚ E5 ⊠ #01-08, Blk 664 Buffalo Road ☎ 296 1838 ⊕ 10–8 ⓜ Bugis MRT

JOSI GEMS

If you're looking for quality loose gems, such as diamonds, emeralds and rubies, this shop is worth a stop.
✚ E6 ⊠ #08-15 Park Mall, 9 Penang Road ☎ 338 7423 ⊕ Mon–Fri 10:30–5; Sat 11–2:30 ⓜ Dhoby Ghaut MRT

LUCKY PLAZA

Many shops here sell freshwater pearls, including choker and bracelet sets. There is a wide variety of colours available, prices depending on the quality and size.
✚ C5 ⊠ 304 Orchard Road ☎ 235 3294 ⊕ 9–9 ⓜ Orchard MRT

MIKIMOTO

Cultured pearls in necklaces, rings and earrings are available in this boutique inside Takashimaya department store. Black pearl rings are another speciality.
✚ C6 ⊠ 2nd floor, Takashimaya, 391 Orchard Road ⊕ 735 1184 ☎ 10–9:30 ⓜ Orchard MRT

NASH JEWELLERY

This store, and its branch in Tanglin Shopping Centre, sells jewellery retail and wholesale. In addition to loose stones, the store custom designs pieces and sells set jewellery.
✚ C5 ⊠ #03-17 Orchard Towers, 400 Orchard Road ☎ 732 2177 ⊕ 9:45–6.45. Closed Sun ⓜ Orchard MRT

PIDEMCO CENTRE

A wide range of shops make up the Singapore Jewellery Mart, spread over two floors at Pidemco Centre.
✚ d/E7 ⊠ 95 South Bridge Road ☎ 539 7721 ⊕ 10:30–6. Closed Sun ⓜ City Hall MRT

POH HENG JEWELLERS

There are several branches of this store, which mainly sells 20-, 22- and 24-carat gold jewellery.
✚ bII/D8 ⊠ #01-17 People's Park Complex, 1 Park Road ☎ 535 0960 ⊕ 11:30–9 ⓜ Outram Park MRT

ROLEX

Rolex watches at prices that guarantee they are the real thing.
✚ C5 ⊠ #01-01 Tong Building, 302 Orchard Road ☎ 737 9033 ⊕ Mon–Fri 9:15–5:15 ⓜ Orchard MRT

TERESE JADE & MINERALS

Sells loose beads and stones – make your own jewellery or have it custom made here. Good-quality lapis, malachite, *cloisonné* beads and jade.
✚ B5 ⊠ #01-28 Tanglin Shopping Centre, 19 Tanglin Road ☎ 734 0379 ⊕ 10–6. Closed Sun ⓜ Orchard MRT

ELECTRICAL & ELECTRONIC GOODS

CHALLENGER SUPERSTORE

Specialises in computer-related products, offering good variety and reasonable prices.

⊞ E7 ⊠ #06-00 Funan Centre, 109 North Bridge Centre ☎ 336 7747 ⏰ 10:30–8 Ⓜ City Hall MRT

COURTS

The top floor of Courts is filled with appliances ranging from washers and dryers to clocks, stereos and cameras.

⊞ Off map to north-west ⊠ 3rd floor, 205 Upper Bukit Timah Road ☎ 468 1355 ⏰ 10–10 🚌 171, 182

ELECTRIC CITY

A one-stop shop in the heart of Orchard Road for everything electric.

⊞ D6 ⊠ #04-17 and #05-03, The Heeren, 260 Orchard Road ☎ 735 7654 ⏰ 11:30–10 Ⓜ Somerset MRT

FUNAN CENTRE

A huge range of computers and accessories, as well as photographic equipment, fill the stores in this busy mall.

⊞ E7 ⊠ 109 North Bridge Road ☎ 336 8327 ⏰ 11–7/8 Ⓜ City Hall MRT

MOHAMED MUSTAFA & SAMSUDDIN CO

All three floors of this shop display a variety of small appliances, stereos, clocks and cameras.

⊞ F5 ⊠ #01-02-03 Serangoon Plaza, 320 Serangoon Road ☎ 298 2967 ⏰ Mon–Fri 9AM–10PM; Sat–Sun 9AM–10:30PM 🚌 66, 67

PARIS SILK

Don't be deceived by the small size of this shop; anything from washers and dryers to cameras can be bought at reasonable prices.

⊞ Off map to west ⊠ 15A Lorong Liput, Holland Village ☎ 466 6002 ⏰ Mon–Sat 11–8; Sun 11–4 🚌 5, 7, 61, 106

PERTAMA MERCHANDISING

Specialises in household appliances, TVs and audio equipment. Branches can be found islandwide.

⊞ D6 ⊠ #03-08 Centrepoint, 170 Orchard Road ☎ 732 8686 ⏰ 10:30–9 Ⓜ Somerset MRT

SIM LIM SQUARE

Several floors of shops sell a large variety of electronic goods, including small appliances, televisions and radios. Watch for those stores displaying the red 'Merlion' logo, a sign certifying this is a 'Good Retailer' approved by the STB. And watch out for the hasslers!

⊞ E5 ⊠ 1 Rocher Canal Road ☎ 336 3922 ⏰ Computer stores: 10:30–6. Electronic stores: 10:30–8:30 Ⓜ Bugis MRT

TANGS

The third floor of this popular department store has shelf after shelf of cameras, televisions and electronic items.

⊞ C5 ⊠ 320 Orchard Road ☎ 737 5500 ⏰ Mon–Fri 11–9; Sat 11–9:30; Sun noon–8 Ⓜ Orchard MRT

Before leaving home

It is said by some that Singapore no longer carries the best prices on electronics. Before leaving home, check the prices and model numbers of the brands you are interested in so as to have a point of comparison when visiting the hundreds of electronics stores here. Most items can be purchased with or without a guarantee; whether you choose to have one may affect the price. Read the guarantee carefully if you do choose one, and make sure the voltage of the item and the wiring and plug fit your requirements at home.

THEATRE, MUSIC & CINEMA

A nation of cinema-goers

Going to the movies is a very popular occupation in Singapore, and cinema complexes have been springing up all over the island in recent years. A great number of English-language films are shown, as well as some Chinese films, usually with English subtitles. In recent years the screening of European and Australian films has also become quite common. Surprisingly, some American films open in Singapore before they reach Europe. At weekends, in particular, it is often necessary to book in advance. One of the largest complexes to open recently is the Orchard Cineleisure Centre on Grange Road (near Somerset MRT). The six cinema screens, video arcade and numerous cafés attract a young crowd.

DRAMA CENTRE

A range of plays is performed here, sometimes by local amateur dramatic groups, of which there are a number in Singapore.
➕ E6 ✉ Fort Canning Road
☎ 336 0005 Ⓜ Dhoby Ghaut MRT

INDIAN DANCE PERFORMANCES

Singapore's Indian population takes its dance very seriously, and there are dance academies which put on public performances. The exacting steps and hand gestures (*mudra*), the exciting rhythms and the brilliant costumes of dance forms such as *orissi* are an unusual delight.

KALLANG THEATRE

This is Singapore's largest theatre; it is here that crowd-pulling shows such as *Cats* are staged.
➕ H6 ✉ Stadium Walk
☎ 345 8488 🚌 16

THE LIDO

There's a wide choice at this new cinema complex in the heart of Orchard Road. One of the cinemas, Lido Classic, screens more serious, arty films.
➕ C5 ✉ Level 5, Shaw House, Orchard Road ☎ 732 4124.
Credit-card bookings: 235 8133
🕐 Ticket sales: 10:30–9:30
Ⓜ Orchard MRT

PICTUREHOUSE

Billed as the city's art-movie house, Picturehouse has the most comfortable seats in Singapore, although the air-conditioning is rather fierce!
➕ E6 ✉ 6 Handy Road
☎ 338 3400 🕐 Ticket sales: 10–8 Ⓜ Dhoby Ghaut MRT

STREET WAYANG

Chinese *wayang*, or opera, is performed from time to time in theatres, but the best place to catch it is in the street. Professional troupes (often from China) still set up makeshift stages in Chinatown and in HDB estates, especially during the month of the Hungry Ghosts (▶ 81).

THE SUBSTATION

The Substation is a small studio-type theatre where modern, and often local, plays are performed. A good café and tiny exhibition space are also packed into the small premises.
➕ E6 ✉ 45 Armenian Street
☎ 337 7800 Ⓜ City Hall MRT

VICTORIA CONCERT HALL

Classical and other music concerts take place here, the official home of the Singapore Symphony Orchestra. The orchestra plays Friday and Saturday (often the same programme) throughout most of the year.
➕ d1/E7 ✉ Empress Place
☎ 337 7490 Ⓜ Raffles Place MRT

VICTORIA THEATRE

This is Singapore's oldest theatre. Drama, dance and music are performed here.
➕ d1/E7 ✉ Empress Place
☎ 337 7490 Ⓜ Raffles Place MRT

BARS & NIGHTCLUBS

BONNE SANTÉ
This fancy wine bar in CHIJMES courtyard is a magnet for Singapore's yuppies.

E6 ✉ #01-13 CHIJMES, 30 Victoria Street ☎ 338 1801 ⏰ Mon–Fri 5PM–1AM; Sat–Sun 6PM–2AM 🚇 City Hall MRT

CHANGI SAILING CLUB
Although a private club and rather a long way out of town, this makes a lovely, relaxing place for an evening drink and meal, which can be taken on the small balcony overlooking the beach, under the palm trees or in the comfortable bar. Non-members are admitted for a dollar during evenings, Monday to Friday.

Off map to north-east ✉ 32 Netheravon Road ☎ 545 2876 ⏰ Restaurant: 10–10 🚇 MRT to Tanah Merah then bus 2

FABRICE'S WORLD MUSIC BAR
The ethnic artefacts, Persian rugs, cushions and sofas add to the atmosphere of this subterranean night spot. It can get very crowded late evening, but is good for a quiet early drink.

D6 ✉ Basement, Marriott Hotel, 320 Orchard Road ☎ 738 8887 ⏰ Mon–Fri 5PM–3AM; Sat, Sun and eve of public hols 7PM–3AM 🚇 Orchard MRT

HARRY'S QUAYSIDE
The riverside location close to the city makes this one of the most popular places for an evening drink, so much so that the clientele frequently spills out on to the pavement outside. Blues jam sessions on Sundays and jazz from 9:30PM Wednesday to Saturday add even more to the bar's appeal.

d1/E7 ✉ 28 Boat Quay ☎ 538 3029 ⏰ Mon–Fri 11AM–midnight; Sat–Sun 11AM–1AM 🚇 Raffles Place MRT

ICE COLD BEER
A noisy, hectic, happening place where the beers are kept on ice under the glass-topped bar.

D6 ✉ 9 Emerald Hill ☎ 735 9929 ⏰ 5PM–midnight 🚇 Somerset MRT

THE LONG BAR
One drink, the gin sling, is usually high on a visitor's list of things to taste in Singapore. However, the re-created Long Bar in Raffles Hotel is a bit low on atmosphere, any old sea dogs having been moved on long ago.

F6 ✉ 2nd Floor, Raffles Hotel Arcade ☎ 337 1886 ⏰ Sun–Thu 11AM–1AM; Fri–Sat 6PM–2AM 🚇 City Hall MRT

THE NEXT PAGE
A spruced-up shop house with trendy décor, and floor cushions and opium beds serving as seating, makes an interesting place to down a few cool beers.

D7 ✉ 15 Mohamed Sultan Road ☎ 235 6967 ⏰ 2PM–3AM 🚇 Dhoby Ghaut MRT 🚌 32, 54, 195

Discos
Some of the city's most popular discos include the following: Fire Disco (✉ #04-19, 150 Orchard Road); Heaven (✉ Orchard Parade Hotel, 1 Tanglin Road); Pleasure Dome (✉ Hotel Phoenix, 277 Orchard Road); and Venom (✉ 12th floor, 9 Pacific Plaza, Scotts Road). Be warned though: they attract a young crowd! Nightclubs such as Fabrice's World Music Bar (see main text) and Zouk's (✉ 17–21 Jiak Kim Street) also have dancing into the early hours.

FESTIVALS & EVENTS

Hong bao

You may notice small red packets on sale in newsagents. These *hong bao*, as they are known, are used for giving gifts of money, particularly for weddings and at Chinese New Year, when it is the custom for unmarried children to receive a red packet. Many employers also choose this time of year to give their red packets – bonuses.

NEW YEAR
(1 JANUARY)
New Year's Day is a public holiday, but it's business as usual for many establishments.

PONGGAL (JANUARY)
The Hindu festival of thanksgiving. As a symbol of prosperity, a pot of rice is allowed to boil over in many homes and offerings are made in temples.

RIVER RAFT RACE
(JANUARY)
All shapes and sizes of rafts race on the Singapore River – and bands, cheerleaders and food stalls are on hand to draw the crowds.

THAIPUSAM
(JANUARY)
To demonstrate their devotion, a few Hindu followers process the 3km from Sri Srinivasa Perumal Temple to Chettiar Temple carrying steel arches (*kavadis*) pinned to them by hooks and skewers which pierce the flesh; some even pull chariots in the same way. These incredible feats of mind over matter occur after days of fasting, and the participants appear entranced and immune to the pain. This festival has been banned in India but continues elsewhere, including Singapore and Malaysia.

RAMADAN
(JANUARY/FEBRUARY)
Ramadan is the month of fasting for Muslims. As night falls and prayers end at the mosques, foodstalls spring up.

HARI RAYA PUASA
(JANUARY/FEBRUARY)
The end of Ramadan and a designated public holiday when Muslim families celebrate together. In the weeks before Hari Raya Puasa a market is held in Geylang – a Malay area – selling traditional delicacies, clothes and household goods.

CHINESE NEW YEAR
(FEBRUARY)
This is Singapore's biggest festival, when families get together to usher in the new year. In the weeks leading up to the two-day public holiday, night markets in Chinatown sell waxed duck, barbecued pork, mandarin orange trees and a million and one joss sticks.

CHINGAY
PROCESSION
(FEBRUARY)
Originally a Chinese folk festival, this secular event has evolved into a huge street carnival. The main stretch of Orchard Road is closed off and a succession of colourful groups parades – lion dancers, acrobats, stiltwalkers, bands and colourful floats – representing all the communities of the city.

VESAK DAY
(USUALLY MAY)
Lord Buddha's birth and enlightenment are commemorated on this day. Although a public

holiday, the festivities are low key. Buddhist *sutras* (scriptures) are chanted by monks at temples and people come to worship and to set caged birds free – gaining merit. In the evening there are candlelit processions.

INTERNATIONAL DRAGON BOAT RACE (JUNE)

Over 20 teams from different countries enter this longboat race, derived from an ancient festival honouring the Chinese poet Qu Yuan.

SINGAPORE FESTIVAL OF ASIAN PERFORMING ARTS (JUNE)

This biennial festival (odd-numbered years) features traditional and classical performances from around the region. There are dance and musical events as well as workshop activities.

NATIONAL DAY (9 AUGUST)

This public holiday marks the anniversary of independence. A huge parade is held in the national stadium, and the festivities end with a spectacular firework and laser display.

FESTIVAL OF THE HUNGRY GHOSTS (AUGUST/SEPTEMBER)

In the seventh month of the lunar calendar it is believed that spirits of the deceased roam abroad. To appease them, offerings are made, rows of incense 'rockets' and joss sticks are lit, and celebratory dinners are held. There are also street *wayang* performances.

MOONCAKE FESTIVAL (SEPTEMBER)

This festival, named after the delicious mooncakes on sale, is a colourful spectacle. In the evenings Chinese lanterns are hung up or carried about by children.

FESTIVAL OF THE NINE EMPEROR GODS (OCTOBER/NOVEMBER)

Over a week-long period, the nine emperor gods, who supposedly can cure illness and grant longevity and good fortune, are thought to visit earth. There are processions and street *wayangs*, and images of the gods are carried on sedan chairs.

THIMITHI (OCTOBER)

Barefoot Hindus walk across a pit of burning coals to show their devotion to Draupathi. At the Sri Mariamman Temple the festival begins early in the morning, with the fire walking at around 5PM.

DIWALI (NOVEMBER)

For the weeks before Diwali, the 'Festival of Lights', Little India is decked in lights to celebrate the triumph of good over evil. Prayers are said and lamps lit in temples and homes.

CHRISTMAS DAY (25 DECEMBER)

Mooncakes

During the mid-autumn festival, mooncakes, which look a little like small meat pies, can be bought from special stalls and at bakeries all over the island. Legend has it that the hero Zhu Yuan Zhang and his followers, in attempts to overthrow the tyrannical Yuan Dynasty in the 14th century, are said to have hidden secret messages inside mooncakes; since then this delicacy has been associated with the festival. The rich pastry cases contain a variety of fillings such as red-bean, lotus-seed and even durian paste; some also contain egg yolks.

LUXURY HOTELS

Prices

Expect to pay over S$300 per night per person at a luxury hotel.

Six-star luxury

Impressively, one of Singapore's newest up-market hotels, the Ritz-Carlton Millennia (✚ F7 ✉ 7 Raffles Avenue ☎ 337 8888 🚇 City Hall MRT), has been termed a 'six-star' hotel. Not surprisingly, it provides all you can imagine in luxury and comfort. With its luxuriously appointed rooms, fine dining, large pool and extensive business facilities, it's ideal for business travellers and for tourists who can afford to splash out. Its commanding position on Marina Bay means there's also the plus of fantastic views over the harbour and civic centre.

FOUR SEASONS

A luxury hotel, ideally located just behind Orchard Road. Top-notch in-room facilities, two pools, air-conditioned tennis courts and good restaurants make this a popular choice.
✚ C5 ✉ 190 Orchard Boulevard ☎ 734 1110 🚇 Orchard MRT

GOODWOOD PARK

Formerly the Teutonia Club (German Club), this hotel has been added to over the years yet still retains much of its charm. It is well located, close to Orchard Road, and also has beautifully landscaped gardens.
✚ C5 ✉ 22 Scotts Road ☎ 737 7411 🚇 Orchard MRT

ORIENTAL

The Oriental is one of three luxury hotels built on reclaimed land overlooking Marina Bay. It is close to the Marina Square shopping centre – good for last-minute gifts – and the newly completed Suntec City, Asia's largest conference and exhibition centre.
✚ F7 ✉ 5 Raffles Avenue, Marina Square ☎ 338 0066 🚇 City Hall MRT

RAFFLES

For those wishing to relive the golden age of travel, a stay at Raffles may be just the ticket, but it's expensive – first class all the way! There are no individual rooms for guests, only suites. Although the main guest areas of the hotel are private, step beyond them and you will, at once, be conscious that you're staying in a major tourist attraction. (► 44)

SHANGRI-LA

One of Singapore's finest hotels, with all the facilities you'd expect from a top-class hotel, plus some magnificent gardens – often described as 'Singapore's other botanic garden'. Sporting facilities include a golf putting green. Dining opportunities are first rate, as is the service.
✚ B5 ✉ 22 Orange Grove Road ☎ 737 3644 🚇 Orchard MRT

SINGAPORE MARRIOTT

A great Singapore landmark, the Dynasty Hotel, was refurbished and then opened for business as the Marriott in 1995. The original distinctive pagoda-roofed tower is still there, forming the hotel. Its central location, above Tangs department store, adds to the appeal.
✚ C5 ✉ 320 Orchard Road ☎ 735 5800 🚇 Orchard MRT

WESTIN STAMFORD

Reputedly the tallest hotel in the world outside America, this luxury hotel has all possible amenities, including good sports facilities and, of course, breathtaking views.
✚ F7 ✉ 2 Stamford Road ☎ 338 8585 🚇 City Hall MRT

MID-RANGE HOTELS

ALBERT COURT HOTEL
This hotel, located near Little India, has good facilities at reasonable prices.
✚ E5 ✉ 180 Albert Street ☎ 339 3939 Ⓜ Bugis MRT

EXCELSIOR HOTEL
Very well located, with Chinatown, the colonial centre and Marina Bay all a stone's throw away. Standard facilities include a swimming pool on the fifth floor.
✚ E5 ✉ 5 Coleman Street ☎ 338 7733 Ⓜ City Hall MRT

GARDEN HOTEL
This pleasant hotel is slightly off the beaten track, but it represents very good value for money, having all the facilities of a five-star hotel including a swimming pool. It is within walking distance of both Orchard and Scotts roads.
✚ C4 ✉ 14 Balmoral Road ☎ 235 3344 Ⓜ Newton MRT

GOLDEN LANDMARK
The Golden Landmark Hotel is situated in the heart of the Arab Street area, just next to Sultan Mosque. It has all the facilities you would expect to find in a large hotel, including a swimming pool.
✚ F6 ✉ 390 Victoria Street ☎ 297 2828 Ⓜ Bugis MRT

HOTEL ASIA
The Asia is very conveniently located, lying equidistant from Newton Circus hawker centre, the MRT and the beginning of the major shopping district.
✚ C5 ✉ 37 Scotts Road ☎ 737 8388 Ⓜ Newton MRT

IMPERIAL
This is a five-star hotel, but a little cheaper than most in Singapore. It is very well located for exploring the main areas of the city – Orchard Road, Chinatown and the colonial centre – and has a fantastic Indian restaurant and a swimming pool.
✚ D6 ✉ 1 Jalan Rumbia ☎ 737 1666 Ⓜ Dhoby Ghaut MRT

ROYAL
The Royal is one of Singapore's older hotels. It is a few minutes' walk from Newton MRT and the famous Newton Circus hawker centre. Facilities include a swimming pool.
✚ D4 ✉ 36 Newton Road ☎ 253 4411 Ⓜ Newton MRT

TRADERS HOTEL
Conveniently located close to the Botanic Gardens and Orchard Road. Includes family apartments with small kitchens, and rooms with fold-away beds that can double as meeting rooms for business travellers.
✚ B5 ✉ 1A Cuscaden Road ☎ 738 2222 Ⓜ Orchard MRT

Prices
Expect to pay between S$150–300 per person per night at a mid-range hotel.

Singapore's only urban resort
Merchant Court Hotel (✚ cl/E7 ✉ 20 Merchant Road ☎ 337 2288 Ⓜ City Hall MRT), located on the Singapore River between Clarke Quay and Chinatown, is a good choice for all types of travellers. Extensive facilities include a great pool, business centre, self-service launderette and a relaxing lobby bar, Crossroads.

BUDGET ACCOMMODATION

Hostels and cheap stays

Singapore, unlike many Asian cities, does not have a plethora of good, cheap accommodation. Some of the places listed on this page charge around S$100 per night per room, and are of a good standard. There are cheaper establishments, especially around Bencoolen Street, and some dormitory-style hostels, known as 'crash pads', but the standards of cleanliness and privacy can be quite low. The STB issues a booklet entitled *Budget Hotels*, which lists a number of places that charge under S$60 per night.

BROADWAY

Its Serangoon Road location puts the Broadway Hotel in the middle of the Little India district. Standards are high and the staff friendly. Good Indian restaurant next door.

✚ E5 ✉ 195 Serangoon Road ☎ 292 4661 Ⓜ Bugis MRT

DAMENLOU

Well located in Chinatown. Rooms are clean (if in need of a little refurbishment), with *en suite* facilities. Restaurant and rooftop terrace.

✚ cIII/E8 ✉ 12 Ann Siang Hill ☎ 221 1900 Ⓜ Outram Park MRT

LITTLE INDIA GUEST HOUSE

Very basic – no *en suite* rooms and no café – but right in the heart of Little India. Recommended for very limited budgets.

✚ E5 ✉ 3 Veerasamy Road ☎ 294 2866 Ⓜ Bugis MRT

MAJESTIC

Refurbishment has stripped this classic backpackers' retreat of its faded charm, but the good-quality facilities, great location on the edge of Chinatown and warm welcome definitely compensate.

✚ aIII/D8 ✉ 31–7 Bukit Pasoh Road ☎ 222 3377 Ⓜ Outram Park MRT

METROPOLE

This fairly new hotel, just over the street from Raffles, is a cut above some of the basic-level hotels. It boasts a good range of facilities and, of course, a prime location!

✚ F6 ✉ 41 Seah Street ☎ 336 3611 Ⓜ Newton MRT

METROPOLITAN YMCA

This is one of a number of YMCAs in Singapore. As the standard is good it is often full, so try to make an advance booking. Restaurant and a swimming pool.

✚ B4 ✉ 60 Stevens Road ☎ 737 7755 Ⓜ Orchard MRT

SAN WAH HOTEL

Very basic hotel in a traditional house. Its cleanliness, low rates and handy location mean that it's always popular.

✚ E6 ✉ 36 Bencoolen Street ☎ 336 2428 Ⓜ Dhoby Ghaut MRT

STRAND

Budget hotel with all the usual facilities – café, *en suite* bathrooms.

✚ E6 ✉ 25 Bencoolen Street ☎ 338 1866 Ⓜ Dhoby Ghaut MRT

YMCA INTERNATIONAL HOUSE

This YMCA has a prime location at the start of Orchard Road. It boasts a swimming pool and restaurant, while the presence of a McDonald's next door ensures Big Macs are offered on the room service menu!

✚ E6 ✉ 1 Orchard Road ☎ 336 6000 Ⓜ Dhoby Ghaut MRT

SINGAPORE
travel facts

ARRIVING & DEPARTING

Passports and visas

- Visas are not required by citizens of the USA, EU or most European and Commonwealth countries. Passports must be valid for six months from the date of entry into Singapore.
- Visas are required by Indian visitors who plan to stay more than 14 days.
- On arrival, tourist visas are issued for 14 days. Extensions are obtainable from the Singapore Immigration Building ⊠ 10 Kallang Road ☎ 1800 391 6400, or by making a trip outside Singapore.

Vaccinations

- No vaccinations are required unless you are coming from an area infected with yellow fever or cholera.
- It is safe to drink tap water and eat from foodstalls and hawkers.

Insurance

- Take out comprehensive insurance: although Singapore is virtually free of attacks, pickpocketing and the like, other areas within the region you may want to visit are not so crime-free.
- Medical charges are quite expensive, so it is as well to be covered.

When to go

- Festivals are held throughout the year, but the most colourful are Chinese New Year and the Mooncake Festival and Festival of the Hungry Ghosts celebrations (► 80–1).

Climate

- The temperature range is pretty steady, from a night-time low of 24°C to a daily high of 33°C throughout the year, though December and January can be slightly cooler and May to August slightly hotter.
- Rainfall is also fairly constant but peaks between November and January with the north-east monsoon. However, it rarely rains for long periods – usually an hour's torrential downpour at a time. During monsoon times these storms can be very dramatic, with sheets of rain falling and intense thunder and lightning. They happen most often early in the morning and during mid-afternoon.
- Humidity can sometimes reach nearly 100 per cent, and averages out at 84.4 per cent.
- In the high temperatures and humidity it is perfectly normal to perspire profusely: remember to take clothes that can easily be washed.

Arriving by air

- Singapore's Changi Airport – probably the cleanest and most efficient in the world – is very well served by flights from all major destinations. Direct flights from Western Europe take around 13 hours.
- Taxi ranks are well marked and there is rarely a queue. The fare into the centre is around S$20.
- The airport bus is much cheaper, at around S$5, and stops at major hotels. Buses 16 and 36 ply from the airport to the city.
- Prior to leaving the customs hall, free telephone calls can be made within Singapore.
- Useful numbers: Customs – Terminal 1 ☎ 542 7058/545 9122, Terminal 2 ☎ 543 0754/543 0755; Changi Airport enquiries ☎ 1800 542 1234/6988; Airbus ☎ 542 1721.

Arriving by bus & coach

- Air-conditioned coaches come direct from Bangkok, Penang and Kuala Lumpur, and from other main towns in the Malay Peninsula. The journey from Penang takes around 14–16 hours, and from KL 6 hours.
- Coaches arrive and depart from Lavender Street coach station.
- Bus 170 leaves Johor Bahru bus station regularly for Queen Street bus station in Singapore. Depending on the traffic on the causeway to Singapore Island, the journey from JB takes around one hour.
- Express service information: Singapore–Johor Bahru Express ☎ 292 8149; Singapore–Malacca Express ☎ 293 5915; Singapore–Kuala Lumpur Express ☎ 292 8254.

Arriving by train

- There is one main train line north–south in Malaysia. Around four trains arrive per day in Singapore from Kuala Lumpur. Journey times vary depending upon whether it is an express service or the mail train.
- Immigration formalities occur once you've disembarked at Singapore's Keppel Road railway station, though it is still technically in Malaysian territory ☎ 222 5165.
- For those with large budgets, the newly introduced Eastern and Oriental Express ☎ 227 2068 offers a leisurely and luxurious trip to Singapore from Bangkok, Penang or Kuala Lumpur.

Arriving by sea

- Most cruise ships put passengers ashore at the World Trade Centre, from where there are buses and taxis into town.

- There are ferries between Tanjong Belungkor (Johor) and Changi ferry terminal (Ferrylink ☎ 545 3600); to and from Pulau Tioman Mar–Oct (Auto Batam Ferries ☎ 542 7105); and between the World Trade Centre and Batam and Bintan (Auto Batam Ferries ☎ 271 4866).

Departure tax

- A departure tax of S$15 is charged at the airport. You can either pay it there or buy a coupon at your hotel in advance.

Customs regulations

- One litre each of spirits, wine and beer can be brought into Singapore duty-free, along with a reasonable amount of personal items and gifts.
- Duty has to be paid on cigarettes, cigars and tobacco.
- A number of items are prohibited, notably weapons, firecrackers, drugs, pornographic and pirated material, certain publications and chewing-gum. Video cassettes may also be subject to inspection.
- There is no limit to the amount of currency you may bring in.

GST

- If you buy goods worth S$300 or more (as three or fewer S$100 purchases) you may, as a visitor, be eligible to claim back the 3 per cent Goods and Services Tax (GST).
- You will need to ask for and fill out a GST Claim Form in the shop. Make sure you have your passport with you whenever you go shopping if you are planning to claim this tax back.
- On departure from Singapore you will need to produce your copy of this form, along with the goods themselves, at special counters at

the airport in order to obtain your GST rebate. Enquiries ☎ 225 6238.

ESSENTIAL FACTS

Opening hours

- Shops: usually Mon–Sat 10–9:30; some do close earlier. Many shops are open on Sunday.
- Banks: Mon–Fri 9–3; Sat 10–12.
- Doctors' clinics: Mon–Fri 9–6; Sat 9–12.

Public holidays

- New Year's Day – 1 January
- Hari Raya Puasa – one day, January/February
- Chinese New Year – two days, February
- Good Friday – March/April
- Hari Raya Haji – one day, April
- Labour Day – 1 May
- Vesak Day – one day, May
- National Day – 9 August
- Diwali – November
- Christmas Day – 25 December

Money matters

- You can change money at the airport on arrival, or at hotels, banks and money-changers. The latter occupy licensed booths all over town and usually offer a fairly standard rate which may be slightly better than that given by banks and hotels.
- Automatic teller machines (ATMs) issue money on credit cards. The most central ones can be found at Raffles City, handily placed just next to the entrance to City Hall MRT station.
- The Singapore dollar and other major currencies are easily changed to the local currency in Malaysia and Indonesia if you go to these countries on excursions.
- Brunei dollar notes have the same value as the Singapore dollar and are accepted everywhere in Singapore.
- Many shops, restaurants and hotels take credit cards.
- Taxi-drivers sometimes may not have sufficient change to accept large notes, so make sure you have some low denomination notes with you.
- Buses take exact change, though you can always give a dollar coin for a journey you know costs less.

Etiquette

- Singapore is a very regulated city, with rules guarding against jaywalking, spitting and littering, among other things. Fines for littering can be about S$1,000, as they can be for smoking in the wrong place. Smoking is prohibited on buses and the MRT, and in taxis, lifts, theatres, cinemas, government offices, air-conditioned restaurants and shopping centres.
- Given the extreme heat and humidity, fairly casual clothes are acceptable in most places, though some clubs and bars do stipulate no shorts.
- Tipping is actively discouraged in Singapore, be it in restaurants, hotels or taxis, though restaurants do charge for service, a goods sales tax and an entertainment tax, which amounts to a total of around 14 per cent. This is often expressed on bills and receipts as '++'.
- When visiting temples, mosques and other places of worship act in a respectful manner: wear appropriate clothing, don't make too much noise and, particularly for Muslim and Hindu places of worship, remove your shoes before entering.
- Muslims (Malays) consider it especially rude to point with your

finger, so try to avoid doing this and use your whole hand instead.

- When eating out with Muslims and Hindus remember that they consider it unclean to eat with the left hand and rarely use cutlery. Muslims do not eat pork and many Hindus are vegetarian.
- Chopsticks are the norm in Chinese restaurants, though spoons and forks will be brought to struggling visitors.
- Eating is almost a national pastime, especially for the Chinese, so don't be surprised if hardly a word is uttered once the food is served. All concentration is devoted to the matter in hand – namely, eating!
- If invited to a Chinese wedding an appropriate gift is a red packet (*hong bao*) containing money – say around S$40.
- At Chinese New Year, should you be invited to someone's home, the gift to take is oranges – but never an odd number, which the Chinese consider unlucky.

Toilets

- There are easily accessible, clean toilets in almost every shopping centre and hawker centre.
- If you are caught short remember that MRT stations also usually have public toilets.
- It is quite acceptable practice to use toilets in hotels, even if you're not staying there.
- Some public toilets charge 10 or 20 cents and will then provide lavatory paper.
- Be prepared to use squatting toilets occasionally, though you will find that most places do offer a choice!

Lone travellers

- There are no special precautions that lone travellers have to take in

Singapore. Indeed, the city is probably one of the safest places in the world for people travelling on their own.

Student travellers

- Accommodation is generally expensive, with cheap options fairly hard to find, though there are budget-priced hostels (▶ 84, panel).
- Food, however, is relatively inexpensive compared with European prices, and a meal at a hawker centre may cost as little as S$5.

Time

- Singapore is 8 hours ahead of Greenwich Mean Time (7 hours during British Summer Time) and 2 hours behind Sydney Standard Time.

Electricity

- Singapore operates on 220–240 volts and most sockets take three-pin plugs. Most hotels will supply an adaptor if you need one for an appliance.
- Singapore is rarely subject to power cuts.

Visitors with disabilities

- Many hotels, shops and sights have facilities for those with disabilities, though, as in many other cities, getting around can sometimes be rather more difficult.
- If you have specific queries about particular problems, contact the National Council of Social Services ☎ 336 1544.

Places of worship

- Anglican: St Andrew's Cathedral ✉ St Andrew's Road ☎ 337 6104.
- Jewish: Jewish Synagogue ✉ Waterloo Street ☎ 336 0692.

- Methodist: Wesley Methodist Church ✉ 5 Fort Canning Road ☎ 336 1433.
- Roman Catholic: Cathedral of the Good Shepherd ✉ Queen Street ☎ 337 2036.
- Details of Muslim and Hindu temples are given in the chapters on the Top 25 Sights (➤ 23–48) and Singapore's Best (➤ 49–60) of this book.

Complaints

- If you wish to complain about the service you have received you can contact either the STB (see below) or the Retail Promotion Centre ☎ 458 6377.

Singapore Tourist Board

- Predictably, Singapore's ultra-efficient Tourist Board produces plenty of free literature about the island and tours. Individual guides can be hired for specialist needs and free sightseeing tours are available for transit passengers – contact the Changi Airport lounge. The Board's main office is at Raffles City ✉ #022-34 Raffles Hotel Arcade ☎ 1800 334 1335 ⏰ 8:30–7.
- Many hotels carry an extensive range of tourist brochures.

- Overseas tourist offices are at: Australia ✉ Level 11, AWA Building, 47 York Street, Sydney, NSW 2000 ☎ 02 9290 2882/8; fax 02 9290 2555 and ✉ 8th Floor, St George's Court, 16 St George's Terrace, Perth, WA 6000 ☎ 009 325 8578; fax 09 221 3864. Canada ✉ The Standard Life Building, 121 King Street West, Suite 1000, Toronto, Ontario M5H 3T9 ☎ 416/363 8898; fax 416/363 5752. New Zealand ✉ 3rd floor, 43 High Street, Auckland ☎ 09 358 1191; fax 09 358 1196. UK ✉ Carrington House, 126–30 Regent Street, London W1R 5FE ☎ 0171 437 0033; fax 0171 734 2191. USA ✉ 590 Fifth Avenue, 12th Floor, New York, NY 10036 ☎ 212/302-4861; fax 212/302-4801

and ✉ 8484 Wilshire Boulevard, Suite 510, Beverly Hills, CA 90211 ☎ 213/852-1901; fax 213/852-0129.

PUBLIC TRANSPORT

MRT

- There are two main Mass Rapid Transit (MRT) lines, running north–south and east–west (see MRT map ➤ 93).
- Trains run between 6AM and midnight.
- Single tickets can be bought, or S$7 tourist souvenir stored-value cards for a number of journeys.
- The Transitlink Farecard is also a stored-value card (minimum value S$10). It can be used on buses as well as on the MRT.
- Tickets can be purchased from machines or from ticket offices, and have to be inserted into machines at the barriers when entering and leaving stations. Remember to take the card with you when you are through the barrier unless it is a single journey ticket, in which case the machine will retain the ticket at the end of your journey.
- At the end of your stay refunds can be obtained on any amount outstanding on stored-value cards.
- Useful numbers: MRT ☎ 336 8900; MRT and bus integration ☎ 1800 779 9366.

Bus

- Bus services are numerous and frequent. Individual tickets can be purchased on the bus (exact change only), or the Transitlink Farecard mentioned above can be used on buses as well.
- Machines at the front of the bus take the card and you need to press a button for the price of your particular journey. If you're

not sure of the amount, ask the bus-driver.

- Singapore Explorer stored-value cards are available for use on the buses only – S$5 for one-day and S$12 for three-day cards. These cards can be purchased at MRT stations.
- A comprehensive bus and MRT timetable, called the Transitlink Guide, can be purchased at newsagents for a few dollars.
- Singapore Bus Service runs a hotline enquiry service 🕒 Mon–Fri 8–5:30; Sat 8–1, providing details of routes. Simply tell them where you are and where you want to go. The number is ☎ 1800 287 2727.

Taxi

- Taxis are usually easily found on Singapore's roads, though during the rush-hour peaks of 8AM–9AM and 5PM–7PM and if it's raining they can be much more difficult to come by.
- Shopping centres, sights and stations usually have taxi ranks, and apart from these designated spots taxis can also be hailed along the road. If a taxi is displaying a light at night it means that it is for hire.
- Most taxis are air-conditioned and comfortable.
- Taxis charge an initial pick-up fare of S$2.40. There are surcharges for taxis hired from the airport, for fares between midnight and 6AM, for bookings made in advance and for journeys via the business district.
- It is best to book taxis for important journeys, such as to the airport, in advance. Some numbers for taxi companies:
  ☎ 552 1111;
  ☎ 552 2222;
  ☎ 552 2828;
  ☎ 481 1211.

Trishaw

- This traditional method of transport is popular with tourists around the centre of town, but do be sure to agree a price in advance.

Car hire

- Car hire is expensive, and given the very good public transport system is not essential.
- If you decide to hire a car remember that it is very expensive to take it into Malaysia (much better to hire one there) and that an area day licence has to be bought to take a car into the central business district during the week and until mid-afternoon on Saturdays.
- Coupons must be displayed in your windscreen in many car parks and designated parking places. Area day licences and books of coupons can be purchased at newsagents and garages. Steep fines will be incurred for failing to display licences and coupons.
- Driving is on the left. A valid international or other recognised driving licence is required.

MEDIA & COMMUNICATIONS

Telephones

- Phone calls within Singapore are very cheap – 10 cents is the charge for a local call.
- Both coin- and card-operated telephones are easy to find. Most restaurants and coffee-shops, as well as most shops and sights, have public phones. They can also be found at MRT stations.
- Comcentre II ☎ 734 9465 🕒 Mon–Fri 8–6; Sat 8–4. Closed Sun, public hols offers private telephone and fax booths

91

for local and international numbers, and charges the official rates.

- Phone cards can be purchased at shops and post offices.
- Calls from some hotels are subject to a 20 per cent surcharge.
- International calls need to be prefixed by 001, and this then followed by the country code.
- Calls to Malaysia from Singapore need to be prefixed by 020 and this then followed by the area code (KL – 3, Johor – 7, Penang – 4).
- Directory enquiries: Singapore numbers ☎ 100; international numbers ☎ 104.

Post offices

- Post office hours do vary, but the post office at 1 Killiney Road is open Mon–Sat 9–9; Sun 9–4:30.
- Stamps can be bought in small shops and hotel lobbies as well as at post offices.
- Postcards and aerogrammes to all destinations cost 50 cents. Standard letter rate to Europe/USA is S$1. Prepaid postcards and aerogrammes are available.
- Poste restante facilities are available at the post office at 71 Robinson Road ☎ 222 8899. Simply address mail 'Poste restante, Singapore'.

TV

- There are three Singapore TV channels – you can find programmes in English on Channels 5 and 12. CNN is available at most hotels.

Radio

- There are a number of local radio stations that play popular music.
- The BBC World Service can be picked up on 88.9MHz.

Newspapers & magazines

- The main English-language dailies are the *Straits Times* and the *Business Times*.
- The *International Herald Tribune* is also available, as is a wide range of local and international magazines and publications.
- All publications are subject to strict government-controlled censorship; some foreign magazines and newspapers may be banned for periods of time if articles in them fall foul of the censorship rules.

EMERGENCIES

Lost property

- Only after checking thoroughly that the item is missing should you call the police ☎ 999.
- For lost credit cards use the following numbers: American Express ☎ 299 8133; Diners Card ☎ 294 4222; MasterCard/VISA ☎ 1800 345 1345; JCB ☎ 734 0096.

Medical treatment

- Singapore's medical system is good, private and on the expensive side.
- Many hotels offer guests a doctor-on-call service.
- You can usually just walk into a doctor's surgery or clinic and ask for treatment.
- If you require hospital treatment you will need to provide proof that you can pay for it.
- The best hospitals are Mount Elizabeth's ☎ 737 2666 and Gleneagles ☎ 473 7222, both of which have emergency departments.
- Most medicines should be available in Singapore, but if you have some very special

requirements either bring enough with you to last for your stay or enquire about their availability before you arrive.

Emergency numbers
- Police ☎ 999.
- Fire ☎ 995.
- Ambulance ☎ 995.

Embassies & consulates
- Australia ✉ 25 Napier Road ☎ 737 9311 🕐 Mon–Fri 8:30–4:30.
- Canada ✉ 80 Anson Road, #14-00 IBM Towers ☎ 325 3200 🕐 Mon–Fri 8–12, 2–4.
- India ✉ 31 Grange Road ☎ 737 6777 🕐 Mon–Fri 9–5:30.
- Indonesia ✉ 7 Chatsworth Road ☎ 737 7422 🕐 Mon–Fri 9–4.
- Ireland ✉ 298 Tiong Bahru Road, #08-06 Tiong Bahru Plaza ☎ 276 8935 🕐 9:30–12:30, 2:30–4.
- Malaysia ✉ 301 Jervois Road ☎ 235 0111 🕐 Mon–Fri 8:30–3:30.
- New Zealand ✉ 391A Orchard Road, #15-06 Ngee Ann City Tower A ☎ 235 9966 🕐 Mon–Fri 8:30–4:30.
- UK ✉ 325 Tanglin Road ☎ 473 9333 🕐 Mon–Fri 8:30–5.
- USA ✉ 27 Napier Road ☎ 476 9100 🕐 Mon–Fri 8:30–5:15.

LANGUAGES

- There are four official languages: English, Mandarin, Malay and Tamil. You will find that English is widely understood and spoken in Singapore.
- There is a wealth of English-language publications, ranging from newspapers to magazines and books.
- Road signs, shop signs, bus destinations, tickets and the like all appear in English, and staff in shops, hotels and at places of interest all speak English.

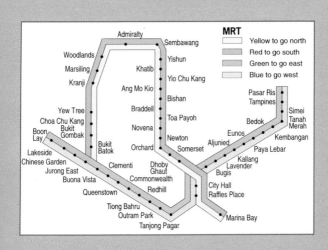

MRT
- Yellow to go north
- Red to go south
- Green to go east
- Blue to go west

Index